The
Connell Guide
to
Shakespeare's

———

Romeo
and
Juliet

———

by
Simon Palfrey

Contents

NOTES

Introduction: the world's greatest love story?

Romeo and Juliet is routinely called "the world's greatest love story", as though it is all about romance. The play features some of the most lyrical passages in all of drama, and the lovers are young, beautiful, and ardent. But when we look at the play, rather than rest in its reputation, the lyricism and the romance are not really what drive things along. It is true that Romeo, especially early on in the play, acts like a young man determined to take his place in an immortal tale of love. Everything he says is romantic – but rather like an anniversary card is romantic. His words propel nothing, or nothing but sarcastic admonitions from his friends to forget about love and to treat women as they should be treated, with careless physical appetite. The world we have entered is rapacious more than romantic.

Everyone knows something of this, from the film versions of the story if nothing else. Romeo and Juliet must fight for their love inside a culture of stupid hatreds. But it is not a simple case of love versus war, or the city against the couple. If it were, it would nicely reinforce clichés about true love, fighting against the odds. I want to suggest that the play Shakespeare actually wrote is more troubling than this. Its lovers oppose the world they are born into: but the nature of their love is also born profoundly from it.

In the first acts of the play, much of the energy and vitality comes from Romeo's friend, Mercutio. He is the most vehemently anti-romantic figure imaginable. He takes the city's over-heated culture of violence, sex and one-upmanship, and accelerates it all into pathological, friend-tiring jokes.

Now we might think it the purpose of Romeo, and the play, to fly beyond Mercutio's sexual revulsion, his verbal fantasies, and to find something whole and true like love. And certainly this is partly what happens. But it doesn't happen in the way we might think it should – by Romeo meeting Juliet, and everything else sliding away into irrelevance. For what happens is that Romeo meets Juliet, and everything is transformed by her: but it is also transferred into her. Not only Romeo's ardour, but the demonic energies of the city and Mercutio, are crystallised and somehow alchemised in Juliet. She turns the lead to gold – bright, hot, the standard of all exchange. But she is also too precious to be safely seen, and fatal to anyone who truly does see her.

Once Romeo properly meets her – in the balcony scene – Juliet takes over the play almost completely (a possession cued by the passing of Mercutio in Act Three, Scene One). Hers is the energy and desire that pushes things to completion. And this appetite is absolutely a thing of violence. Juliet takes her place as a characteristic Shakespearean hero, one who feels a passion or sees a possibility and drives through to its satisfaction, whatever the cost. Her passion – for all her youth, for all its truth – is at the very cusp of murderousness.

There is one moment in the play which exemplifies this passionate pitilessness. It is when Juliet has agreed to take the sleeping potion. She goes to her nurse, and her mother, and her father, and solemnly swears that she now agrees with their wishes for her, that she will confess her sins (of disobedience) and marry Paris as they have bid her. She gets her parents' thanks and blessing, and leaves to her bedchamber. She does so knowing they will never see her again.

The heart thrills and freezes at the thought. Could there be an act colder in its heat, more open-eyed in its annihilation of everything that until this day has most mattered?

The Prince, at the end of the play, blames the families for the deaths of the young lovers ("See what a scourge is laid upon your hate"). But this strikes me as false, almost as a kind of bad faith. Of course the things that the families do force the lovers' hands. But as much as such plot-devices are at work, they are used to trigger events – Romeo's exile, Juliet's sleeping potion, and so on – rather than define their substance. The truly substantial thing is whatever moves, or moves in, its heroine. For Juliet represents the devastating coming-true, for better and worse, of everything in this world. She is its scourge, in the sense that she will whip and punish and haunt it; she is also its triumph, in the sense of its best and truest thing. The deaths it all leads to are in no way avoidable, and in no way accidental. They are her inheritance, the thing she was born to. Of course she takes Romeo with her. But it is at heart her play.

THE CHARACTERS

JULIET
CAPULET, *her father*
LADY CAPULET, *Capulet's wife*
TYBALT, *her nephew*
ESCALUS, *prince of Verona*
COUNT PARIS
MERCUTIO
MONTAGUE
LADY MONTAGUE
ROMEO
BENVOLIO, *Montague's nephew*
THE NURSE
FRIAR LAURENCE
PETER, SAMPSON, *serving men of the Capulets*
Gregory, Friar John, an Apothecary, Abraham, Balthasar, a Chorus

A summary of the plot

Act One

A brawl breaks out in Verona's streets. Once again it is the men of the feuding noble families of Capulet and Montague. Prince Escalus intervenes, declaring that further fighting will be punishable by death.

Paris, a kinsman of the Prince, talks to Lord Capulet about marrying Juliet, Capulet's 13-year-old daughter. Her father invites him to a ball. Juliet is unconvinced.

Romeo, son to Montague, missed the brawl. His family and friends wonder where he is. He tells of his unrequited love for Rosaline, and is persuaded to attend the Capulet ball, disguised by a mask, in the hope of meeting Rosaline. Instead he meets and falls in love with Juliet.

Act Two

After the feast, Romeo overhears Juliet on her balcony confessing her love for him. They agree to marry in spite of their families' hatred. With the help of Friar Laurence, they are secretly married the next day. No one else knows except Juliet's Nurse.

Act Three

Tybalt, Juliet's cousin, challenges Romeo to a duel. Romeo refuses to fight. Romeo's friend Mercutio fights instead, and is fatally wounded when Romeo attempts to break up the duel. In a rage, Romeo kills Tybalt.

The Prince exiles Romeo on pain of death. Romeo secretly spends the night in Juliet's chamber. The next morning the lovers part. Capulet, believing Juliet's grief to be caused by Tybalt's death, insists that she marry Paris immediately. The Nurse recommends bigamy, and Juliet feels betrayed. Now she is on her own.

Act Four

In despair, Juliet consults Friar Laurence. He bids her to pretend to consent to the match with Paris, but on the night before the wedding to drink a potion that will make her comatose for "two and forty hours". His plan is for Romeo to rescue her from the family crypt and carry her to Mantua.

The next morning the Nurse discovers her apparently dead. Her family wail and mourn. She is entombed according to plan. But Friar Laurence's message to Romeo doesn't arrive in time.

Act Five

Romeo is told that Juliet is dead. He buys poison and returns to the Capulet crypt. There he meets Paris, who has also come to mourn Juliet. Romeo kills Paris. Still believing Juliet to be dead, he kisses her and drinks the poison. Juliet awakes and, finding Romeo dead, stabs herself with his dagger. Faced with this sorry sight, the fathers agree to end their violent feud.

What is the play about?

If *Romeo and Juliet* is a play about passion, it is implicitly one of rebellion. This is the key to its extraordinary magnetism. Not a rebellion of people against the state, or not in any simple way. Rather, it is a play about the rebellion of the heart, our basic vitality, a thing equally of spirit and body, against all forms of false, complacent, begrudging, insensible constriction. It is a play that taps into the desire, cherished by all of us, for a life less afraid, less timid and obedient, less, in a very basic way, predicted.

Shakespeare's play knows what an awful thing it is to know everything that must follow from the fact of our birth here, now, among these people and those institutions. How deadening to think that we have, in truth, no choice in what follows at all – that even our thoughts and emotions are likewise already scripted, waiting for us to rehearse and perform them. Thought is free? Not here it isn't – not in Shakespeare's Verona! We even know who we are to hate, and who we can share our hatreds with. Who would not rebel against such a world? Who would not rebel to love's side! *

Romeo and Juliet strikes upon that little flint in us all, what the philosophers sometimes call our 'conatus'. We might call it the soul's appetite – the

*As Marx said, "The tradition of the dead generations weighs like a nightmare on the minds of the living."

10

sense that life is abundant, or should be; that we are born to strive, and that our identity, our being, is a purposive force, searching always for some opportunity or other to strike us into flaming completion; that what might or should or may be really could be. William Hazlitt calls Shakespeare the poet of what would be, of what if – and this is what Juliet and Romeo live. They turn cannot into would. They make the impossible possible.

Romeo and Juliet, then, is a play about the inadequacy of what is habitually given and accepted as our daily lot; about the consequent need, if life and language are to be authentic, for rebellion or internal exile. The Shakespeare critic Kiernan Ryan puts it like this:

> *Romeo and Juliet* lays siege to the legitimacy of a world which deprives men and women of boundless love as surely as it deprives the poor of their share in the worlds' wealth, seeing the lovers as born before their time, citizens of an anticipated age... marooned in a hostile, alien reality, which has already contaminated their hearts and minds, and eventually crushes them completely.

The play is equally about the inevitability of failure, because the institutions of their world, as currently constituted, are immovable. It is about the humiliation of mere survival, and the transformative promise given to us, the witnesses, who through feeling so passionately for the condemned lovers forswear any timid, paltry, obedient kind of survival. In its place, we imaginatively allow only the kind of survival that is willing to endure death as the price of truth and passion – to witness it and live somehow in it.

How does *Romeo and Juliet* differ from Shakespeare's comedies?

The premise of the Oscar-winning *Shakespeare in Love* was that *Romeo and Juliet* began its life as a comedy. The same idea has regularly occurred to critics of the play, who identify a basically comic world until the moment when Mercutio is slain and everything is suddenly doomed. Before that, the argument goes, the action comes straight from comi-romantic cliché: the hero and heroine, paragons of youth and hope and health, falling in love in defiance of foolishly censoring authority. This view is well articulated by Susan Snyder's *The Comic Matrix of Shakespeare's Tragedies* (1979):

> Comedy is organised like a game... *Romeo and Juliet*, young and in love and defiant of obstacles, are attuned to the basic movement of the comic game toward marriage and social regeneration. But

they do not win: the game turns into a sacrifice, and the favoured lovers become victims of time and law.

But is this to say that *Romeo and Juliet* is essentially about escapist desire, only with the catch that, as Snyder has it, "comic adaptability confronts tragic integrity", meaning that only the elders survive into the future whereas, in comedy, it is the young and marriageable?

Most of Shakespeare's comedies turn on similar questions of obedience to the law of the elders. The heroine is confronted by patriarchal obstinacy – a law, a will of one kind or another, an obtuse failure on the part of the parent truly to see what is before them: typical examples are Portia hemmed in by the "will" of her dead father's caskets in *The Merchant of Venice*, or the escape into the forest away from forbidding patriarchy in *A Midsummer Night's Dream* and *As You Like It*. The woman's resistance or exile is ours. This resistance speaks for everything that is intelligent, sensitive to feeling, in touch with necessary futures. Of course the heroines of comedy are not perfect. They can be foolish or ungenerous or too quick to judge. In a number of plays Shakespeare introduces heroines who seem already suspicious of male appetite, and neurotically or violently defended against it. We see this with Katherina in *The Taming of the Shrew*, Beatrice in *Much Ado About Nothing*, Isabella in *Measure for Measure*. But in these cases just as much as the others, the stories revolve around freedom of choice and overcoming false repression, whether internal or external. Where there is a resolution, it hinges upon the heroine discovering, however surprisingly or accidentally, her free choice in love. The infamously difficult ending of *Measure for Measure* – when the Duke mugs the silent Isabella with a sudden marriage proposal – is unsettling partly because we cannot know what degree of choice Isabella has in the matter, but also because we have had no choice in it either. The story has not established the Duke and Isabella as potential lovers; there is no build-up of desire or expectation which the ending can finally satisfy. For all comedy's sometimes carnival exuberance, its satisfactions depend upon tight logic, publicly verified unions, and the agreed granting of permission by both characters and audience.

So how do these examples differ from *Romeo and Juliet*? Is it simply that conventional comedies allow a reconciliation of desire and authority, and *Romeo and Juliet* does not? That the comedies show authorities learning from their mistakes and – unlike *Romeo and Juliet* – the lovers surviving to enjoy the benefit? Or that, again unlike *Romeo and Juliet*, the betrothal that celebrates desire is public rather than secret, and therefore capable of growth?

These things are true, but they do not explain anything. The answer does lie, I think, in how *Romeo and Juliet*'s ending differs from the endings of the comedies – but more profoundly than the above descriptive summaries allow. For the crucial point is that in the comedies we always know the ending before we begin. We know it the whole way through; the ending is immanent in every moment. Now, there may be interesting questions about exactly what the ending of a comedy is: betrothal or marriage, yes, but on what or whose terms, and with what kind of promise, is often open to doubt. Do we return to the beginning, with everything in due patriarchal order, as though the exciting experiments of the plot never were? Or do we perhaps nod along with the tidy ending, whilst identifying the real promise in the new possibilities that the heroines discovered before this formal return to the fold?

Either way, the ending in a comedy – togetherness and survival, a survival premised upon a workable, fertile union between young men and women – is present and at work in every moment of the play, implicitly directing our responses as we cheer on or laugh with or fear for the parties. This means that desire, in Shakespearean comedy, is always directed toward the social world, something shareable and surviving. This does not preclude stark carnality, any more than it does deceit. But such things are counters in a plot, characterising this character or that moment. The main thing is that life goes on for all of us, for richer or poorer, in sickness and in health. The closing betrothal is really a way of saying just this.

As Samuel Johnson said back in the 18th century, Shakespeare's natural bent was probably for comedy. But he knew, always, that comedy is evasive. He knew that there is something just a little, if not depressing, then de-adrenalising about the conventional comic ending. It is satisfying, no doubt, to see the warring lovers united, or mistakes rectified. But that is also the limitation. It seems to satisfy; we have received what we came for. Comic closure is a stopper upon the bottle of thought – and, perhaps, of desire. The typical comedy shows the genie of restlessness roaming around, getting away with what is usually accounted trouble – but the end of the play has the genie back inside the bottle. Shakespeare's comedies, however, are famous for not being entirely resolved; there is always somebody that cannot or will not enter the magic, conflict-dissolving circle. I have mentioned Isabella in *Measure for Measure*, but even the happier endings have their refusers: Malvolio in *Twelfth Night*, Don John in *Much Ado About Nothing*, Shylock, of course, in *The Merchant of Venice*. Even *A Midsummer Night's Dream* ends with one of the lovers, Demetrius, still deceived by the love-potion into loving a besotted woman he has always loathed.

All of this points to something conditional about the satisfaction that these comedies deliver.

At a glance: how Shakespeare changed his source

ARTHUR BROOKE'S *TRAGICALL HISTORYE OF ROMEUS AND JULIET*	SHAKESPEARE'S *ROMEO AND JULIET*
Mercutio...hardly figures... All we are told about him is that he has "cold hands"	*Mercutio... one of Shakespeare's most extraordinary creations*
Romeo walks by Juliet's house for "a week or two in vain" before he speaks to her.	*This is concentrated into one soliloquy, with Juliet already present.*
After their exchange of marriage vows, Romeo and Juliet go straight to Juliet's room and sleep together. He hates the idea of leaving his wife behind	*Between exchanging marriage vows and sleeping together is a street fight, in which Mercutio and Tybalt are murdered; sex is shadowed by death.*
Their love affair is two months long... Brooke writes at length about their time together: "the virgin fort hath warlike Romeo got"	*Their love affair only really lasts for a night*
The Friar gives exceedingly long lectures, some of them 160 lines or more.	*The Friar is not quite so long-winded*
The Nurse calls Juliet a "wyly wench" moved by "lust"	*Juliet is never called such things by anyone, and we are not asked to judge her for it*

Shakespeare never lets the possessors (of grace, love etc.) simply get away with it. He knows that the resolution is partly a lie. He knows that marriage can neither contain nor harness the energies that have propelled the action of the play. Marriage settles the desire, as a lagoon or reservoir might gather the overflowing turbulence of sea. But it is also only marriage, and will not bear too much scrutiny. If Shakespeare had wanted to explore marriage he would have entered a different genre entirely, the cuckold comedy beloved of many of his contemporaries. But the daily business of marriage was always something the great man preferred to keep at a distance.

The satisfactions of comedy-desire are essentially prudential. They speak of prudent negotiation, artful turning away, a willingness not to insist upon too much. If we look for a future these endings dissolve before our eyes. For what in fact are we celebrating at the end of a comedy? Not the serendipity of meeting, or a workable union, or the promise of a decent life, or future children, or the good stock and generous community from which the couples arise, or even hope – the things we might, on a generous construction, identify as the theme of a wedding. Instead, in a comedy we reach a kind of island, or dry land, where hunger is for the moment simply agreed to be assuaged. But hunger, of course, will return.

Romeo and Juliet is different from this. There is nothing prudential about it. It is never an almost-comedy. The story is always mortgaged to death. The prologue tells us this, with its famous introduction to the "star-crossed lovers"; so does the famous title; so does the simple fact that it is a "Tragedy". But above all it is the fierce separateness of Juliet, and Romeo in her wake, from the adult social world that sends the play into orbits far beyond the permissions of comedy. Any critical attempt to socialise the lovers is false. The American scholar Coppelia Kahn sees the play being "about a pair of adolescents trying to grow up. Growing up requires that they separate themselves from their parents by forming with a member of the opposite sex an intimate bond which supersedes filial bonds." This sounds very understanding, but surely it is too much a normalising rationalisation, offered as though to cheer up fearful parents ("all kids act like this, don't worry...").

Jonathan Goldberg comments that "at the end of [Kahn's] ideal trajectory lies the transformation of the couple into its parents; what they rebel against is also what they become. These blandly descriptive sentences reek of prescriptiveness." Let's be clear: all kids do not act like Juliet and Romeo; and these lovers will never turn into anyone's parents. And it is just this that makes them so thrilling.

For, as we shall see, death is present in almost every moment of this play. It is not simply an end, a final punctuation mark or clearing of the stage. Death is the experience and location of the two lovers: it is the space of their love, as much as its destiny. This is something that operatic translations of the story know very well. In Berlioz's version the lovers' words and passion are turned into orchestral music rather than arias or dialogue: their essence is to be beyond individuality. Similarly, Wagner's version of the story, *Tristan und Isolde*, reaches its climax with Isolde's "Liebestod", her love-in-death song, which can only happen once her beloved is dead. The consummation is absolute: the lovers die.

In a fundamental sense that is what *Romeo and Juliet* are always doing. The pun "to die" – meaning to have sex or experience orgasm – was one of the most hackneyed of all in Shakespeare's time. But *Romeo and Juliet* makes the pun come true. That is the difference between this tragedy and any comedy. In comedy, a joke serves the situation, like a little accident. Likewise, in comedy the marriage signifies forgetfulness, a sort of amnesiac continuation. In *Romeo and Juliet* everything is different: the marriage happens halfway through, and the lovers are forever trying to catch-up with its promise; they never joke about sex, because its stakes are far too huge and close; nothing gets left behind; nothing is forgotten.

THE CRITICS ON ROMEO

Romeo has always had a worse press than Juliet, usually because he is seen as a belated, derivative figure, drawing his light and fire from some other source (Petrarch, Mercutio, Juliet). His motions, therefore, are reactive, always in danger of being either premature or belated. Here are three 19th-century views of him that put the Romeo "problem" starkly but clearly:

I consider Romeo designed to represent the character of an unlucky man – perpetually so unfortunate as to fail in every aspiration, and, while exerting himself to the utmost in their behalf, to involve all whom he holds dearest in misery and ruin.

...when looking on the timeless tomb of Romeo, and contemplating the short and sad career through which he ran, we cannot help recollecting his mourning words over his dying friend, and suggest as an inscription over the monument of the luckless gentleman,

"I THOUGHT ALL FOR THE BEST."

William Maginn, the colourful contributor of the "Shakespeare Papers" to Charles Dickens' Bentley's Miscellany

He is himself only in his Juliet; she is his only reality, his heart's true home and idol. The rest of the world is to him a passing dream.

William Hazlitt, author of The Characters of Shakespeare's Plays *(1817) a comprehensive account of Shakespeare, play by play, which sold out within six weeks.*

The woman who gives up her whole being to Love rises above the weakness of her sex to the dignity and heroism of a purely human ideality; the man to whom Love becomes the one aim of life, swallowing up all else, resigns himself with riven sails and without helm to the storm. Fallen away from the fundamental law of his being, he presents the unhandsome appearance of all that is discordant and contradictory...

F. Kreyszig, 1859 (Variorum 459)

Kreyszig's critique sounds old-fashioned, but it does point to something that half-cripples Romeo as a would-be transcendent hero. For it speaks volumes about the social pressure on men to be men, to please their fellow menfolk before all others, to take their cues from them, govern their passions as they govern society, to not let down the boys. Of course Romeo tries to advertise his freedom from the gang. But he is always called back.

Why is Romeo introduced to us indirectly?

The first scene displays the infantile boastfulness of Verona's men. Every move is programmed, as though pre-scripted, and then laboriously brought forth. The violence too is belated, and fatally detached from true will or purpose. The brawl seems to be no more than an extension of compulsory male boredom, or libidinal competitiveness. This is true of all of them: the slow-witted servants who first enter; the two patriarchs, buzzing with frustrated male rage like two maddened wasps, held back and drily mocked by their wives; even the earnest Benvolio, as he tells anyone who cares to listen of his own lonely melancholy.

It is clear that the public world of Verona is selfish and violent, ruled by vanity and private grudges. We might think that this is a world requiring the outlet of soliloquy, with its clarity and immediacy. We know that Romeo has not taken part in the affray. It would therefore have been the easiest thing to introduce Romeo alone, speaking his sincerities as a blessed corrective to all the nonsense. But Shakespeare does not do this. Instead, our first sight of Romeo comes through the report of his cousin Benvolio. Suddenly we are in an entirely different world

– the scene truly has changed.

Madam, an hour before the worshipp'd sun
Peer'd forth the golden window of the east
A troubled mind drive me to walk abroad
Where underneath the grove of sycamore
That westward rooteth from this city side
So early walking did I see your son.
Towards him I made, but he was ware of me,
And stole into the covert of the wood.
I, measuring his affections by my own,
Which then most sought where most might not
be found,
Being one too many by my weary self,
Pursu'd my humour, not pursuing his,
And gladly shunn'd who gladly fled from me. [1.1]

Shakespeare gives us here a new scene inside the physically present one – a new place (the woods to the west of Verona), an earlier time (before dawn, threatened by the sun in the east), and a very particular Romeo. It is important that we are introduced to this Romeo before any other. There is as yet nothing to contradict this image, nothing to disabuse us of the impressions it gives or of the trust that it elicits. In this it is like the early allusion to "young Hamlet", before he actually appears, ripe with promise to bring

N.B. All quotations are taken from Arden Shakespeare's 1980 edition clarity to the ghostly night.

But Romeo is not absent only from us. He also escapes from Benvolio. Romeo appears to us, then, in the form almost of a furtive hind, fleeing from pursuers into the perilous safety of the wood. He is glimpsed but not heard; he explains nothing. What we see, then, is Romeo turning away, or Romeo askance, like a mask, or a face half-hidden. The hints of the hunt make him close to us, protected by us. The sense that he is being hunted makes us

BENVOLIO

According to the well-known "type" of the hero's loyal confidante, Benvolio should be merely the bearer of news about Romeo. But he attempts to be the subject of his news as well. So, prone to an unexplained "troubled mind", and then revising his story halfway through, he is exposed as hopelessly self-interested, even in his claim to be "one too many even by my weary selfe". Even melancholy is a form of showing off, not to be trusted, another vein of male competitiveness: hence his need to reassert his wish to be alone in the face of Romeo's rejection. But Shakespeare surely knows that we don't particularly care about Benvolio, neither here nor later. He only exists to shade, accompany, or question Romeo (or elsewhere Mercutio). Shakespeare's interest is in representing a layered social world, in which even private motives are borrowed and imitative. Benvolio's self-excuses are another example of unearned emotion, passion with no source but infectious, affected manners. ◆

feel protective towards him. It as if, at this point, he is no more than a myth, he has a potential that is not quite chartered by available agendas or social grids. If Romeo had acknowledged Benvolio in the woods, it would be as though to say "we are alike". The effect would be to blunt any edge of newness and danger, assure all and sundry that there is nothing to fear in Romeo's un-at-homeness, for he will return. This, of course, is exactly what his first conversation with Benvolio does, with all of its shared bonhomie and second-hand conceits. But in this first glimpse of Romeo, his refusal of exposure or recognition establishes an integrity that male camaraderie, with its habitual coarsening of emotional singularity, cannot touch.

Montague soon augments Benvolio's report with similar fancies, casting the hero as a restless spirit of nature:

> *Many a morning hath he there been seen,*
> *With tears augmenting the fresh morning's dew,*
> *Adding to clouds more clouds with his deep*
> *sighs;*
> *But all so soon as the all-cheering sun*
> *Should in the farthest east begin to draw*
> *The shady curtains from Aurora's bed,*
> *Away from light steals home my heavy son*
> *And private in his chamber pens himself,*
> *Shuts up his windows, locks fair daylight out*
> *And makes himself an artificial night. [1.1]*

In introducing Romeo, Shakespeare's aim is not naturalistic description or even character-consistency. Images are speaking through Romeo's cousin and father, rather than being spoken by them. Shakespeare is laying the groundwork for myth. The pictures work a little like dumbshows, distilling ideals and predicting what shall happen. They articulate a promise that we wait for Romeo fully to inhabit.

What do we make of Romeo's first appearance?

It is crucial to how the play works that Romeo should only come true, as it were, upon meeting Juliet. And so it is that when first we actually meet him he is not fully present. He fails completely to live up to the image we have of the glimpsed figure in the wood; instead of the outsider at odds with his world we see someone behaving and talking like the conventional spurned lover.

Productions sometimes deal with Romeo's disappointing first scene by radically cutting it – hinting at his disaffection but leaving Benvolio and indeed the audience still waiting for an explanation. He is lovelorn and enigmatic – and suitably heroic. This is the solution, for instance, of both the Zeffirelli and Luhrmann films. But in the play itself, Shakespeare does not shy away from Romeo at all. He lets him converse at length – and reveal himself as utterly symptomatic of the corrupted social world. Everyone wills, everyone wants, but inauthentically: their terms are borrowed, or unearned. Here we might think of Rene Girard's theory of mimetic desire:

> To say that our desires are imitative or mimetic is to root them neither in their objects [the one desired] nor ourselves [the one desiring] but in a third party, the model or mediator, whose desire we imitate in the hope of resembling him or her.

Accordingly, Romeo's speech is hackneyed, imitative, and evading of true humanity. His love-paradoxes are no less boastful, no less slow and static, than the banalities of the servants before the fracas: "O heavy lightness, serious vanity", "Feather of lead, bright smoke, cold fire, sick health". Shakespeare is laying it on pretty thick here, advertising how much his hero is in hock to romantic poetic cliché, and specifically the 1590s vogue for love sonnets established by Queen Elizabeth's cousin, Sir Philip Sidney, with his sonnet sequence *Astrophel and Stella*. To the extent that Romeo's words mean anything more than the fact of such imitation, they ironically describe him: his fire is cold, his health sick, his vanity very serious, a true "misshapen chaos of wellseeming forms". That Shakespeare has got Romeo's vanity in his sights is made very clear by his comical self-forgetfulness immediately after he has first confessed his love (for Rosaline – as yet unnamed) and pondered philosophically upon its tyranny:

> *Alas that love whose view is muffled still*
> *Should without eyes see pathways to his will.*
> *Where shall we dine? [1.1]*

He sounds like one of Bassanio's rich mates in *The Merchant of Venice*, tasting the trials of love like he might a nice little aperitif. All pleasures here are evacuated, integrities mortgaged to the compulsory ideology; all passion is etiolated, like a sick and colourless hothouse plant. We seem to be given a world that derives from elsewhere, full of hollow men echoing clichés, sourced in a common pond that everyone has already fished. We are left waiting for the real thing, for "real fire" rather than the "sick health" of Romeo, Sampson, Tybalt, and the already-ineffectual patriarchs (prince and parents). We are waiting, of course, for Juliet.

How is Juliet introduced?

Scene Two has Juliet introduced, just as Romeo was introduced in Scene One. Again, she is not given to us directly. We hear her by report. She is being bargained for – Paris has a suit to marry her, and her father is, initially at least, reluctant to hand her over. She is only 13, and all his other children have died. Paris asks him, "But now my Lord, what say you to my suit?" – cutting to the chase – and Capulet replies:

> *But saying o'er what I have said before*
> [telling us to listen]
> *My child is yet a stranger in the world,*
> *She hath not seen the change of fourteen years [1.2]*

Paris protests that "Younger than she, are happy mothers made", to which Capulet responds, "And too soone mar'd are those so early made". He rhymes, but the perfection of the rhyme (made/made) is not calming. The word "made" seems too easy to say, too glib in Paris's mouth: "made", after all, is no neutral word. In repeating it Capulet insists on the word's possibilities: it might mean deflowered; it might pun on the loss of maid-enhood, and so the violent paradox of a mother and a maid; more centrally, "made" means finished, completed, done. With this Capulet returns to the point so delicately suggested by "My

Child is yet a stranger in the world": "Earth hath swallowed all my hopes but she,/She's the hopeful Lady of my earth", before abruptly shifting, with "But woo her gentle Paris..." into a long sequence of couplets consenting to the match, if Juliet approves, and announcing the ball that may facilitate it. The 22 line, 11 couplet sequence escapes entirely from inwardness and pain and even memory. We return to the social world, to externals and expediency – that is, to the world we saw in the opening duels and banter. Juliet, in this world, is nothing more than an object for the eye, one among many ("hear all, all see:/And like her most, whose merit most shall be"). She is not essentially present at all.

But there is more than one story going on here, and the public narrative drive is not necessarily the one we most cherish. Capulet has already given us an image of Juliet that – like our glimpse of Romeo in the wood – is powerfully separate from the mundane, male-directed imperatives all around. In this image, Juliet is delicate, vulnerable, unfinished: "my Child is yet a stranger in the world". She is like someone from a Coleridge or Wordsworth ballad, the Child or Stranger, bringing knowledge from elsewhere but unfit for here and now. The sense is that she has been initiated into mysteries; she is of some other substance or material to other mortals; she is constitutionally homeless. Where is she from, we might ask, this

Claire Danes and Leonardo DiCaprio in Baz Luhrmann's 1996 Romeo+Juliet

new arrival? Where is she going?

But if this un-named "she" is somehow un-at-home in this world, she is also the powerfully necessary agent of any hope or redemption: "Earth hath swallowed all my hopes but she,/She's the hopeful Lady of my earth," says her father. She seems to take up the promise of those who are buried, but then she is equally "of" the buried element. Capulet's "earth" is only tenuously above ground: it is premised on premature death, specifically on children's death. It is this that she is the "Lady" of, as though a visitant from elsewhere, a Queen of the endless night. Taken in this way, as a "stranger in the world", Juliet is a refugee from these other realms. She is only visiting, she will not stay among us long. For of course this introduction is ominous. She will soon appear, but only to disappear. Juliet is as fated to die by this introduction as Romeo is by his. He goes to his coffin chamber; she is immediately consigned to "earth".

That she is not yet named is crucial to what Shakespeare is doing. Neither Capulet, Paris, nor of course Romeo, speak the name "Juliet". The "Juliet" we await, then, both is and is not Capulet's daughter and Paris's love-target. Romeo's present beloved was likewise not named (it is only later that we hear of Rosaline). At this preparatory stage in the play, Rosaline and Juliet are at once the same person – as ideals without names or faces – and not the same person (as defined social individuals). Ideal images of love or integrity are everywhere in the air, but also in danger of being traded away, whether by cheap second-hand conceits or the flesh market of male entertainment. No one has yet arrived truly to claim the ideal and bring it home. Still we await Juliet.

But even when we actually see her, Juliet is still partially obscured by others. Juliet's first scene is dominated by the Nurse's long speeches about her as a baby:

> *But as I said,*
> *On Lammas Eve at night shall she be fourteen.*
> *That shall she; marry, I remember it well.*
> *'Tis since the earthquake now eleven years,*

And she was wean'd – I never shall forget it –
Of all the days of the year upon that day...
                    ...But as I said,
When it did taste the wormwood on the nipple
Of my dug and felt it bitter, pretty fool,
To see it tetchy and fall out with the dug...
And since that time it is eleven years.
For then she could stand alond, nay, by
                    th'rood,
She could have run and waddled all about;
For even the day before she broke her brow,
And then my husband – God be with his soul,
'A was a merry man – took up the child,
"Yea," quoth he, "dost fall upon thy face?
Thou wilt fall backward when thou hast more
                    wit,
Wilt thou not, Jule?" And by my holidame,
The pretty wretch left crying and said "Ay".
To see now how this jest shall come about. [1. 3]

One effect of the Nurse's garrulous nativity tales is, almost physically, to surround and overwhelm Juliet. The Nurse lays claim to her nursing and, as though because of this, to her future. This allows Juliet no space beyond the confines in which Nurse and Mother (more or less explicitly, depending on the production) fight for possession of the foundling. The inevitable effect is to make us side with Juliet. Even if we relish the Nurse's tale, we recognise its oppressiveness – how many times has Juliet been subjected to her own story! And here is her Mother, telling her to think on marriage, as she herself had to, at 13 years of age...*

In the midst of all this Juliet has but two brief lines, one begging for peace, the other resisting thoughts of marriage. Rather like our introduction to Hamlet, silent in black amid the loquacious finery of the Elsinore court, Juliet compels our attention, our hungry sympathy, by the simple fact that Shakespeare doesn't give her words to speak. Her elders presume to speak for her – and we all know that elders can never do this adequately. Of course we are fond of the little baby described by the Nurse, weaned and waddling about. But this is not what the Nurse's speech, or Juliet's first scene,

*Everett writes of the Nurse's account of the earthquake: "Because the Nurse is stupid she stands outside of what she sees, endowing [the events] with a curious objectivity... the events... detach themselves from her and animate themselves into a natural history of human infancy. Confused and unjudged, earthquake and weaning interpenetrate in the past, sudden event with slow process: the earthquake becomes necessary, a mere process of maturing, and the weaning of a child takes on magnitude and terribilita, it shakes nature...The Nurse's speech presents an image of Juliet's past that happens to contain, or that contains with a purpose, a premonitory comment on her future...Her speech establishes a natural milieu in which earthquake and weaning, a fall and a being taken up so balance that the ill effects of either are of no importance; and in so far as what she says relates to the rest of the play, it helps to suggest that the same might be true of love and death. And there seems to be a peculiar echo of her procedure in all the rhetorical doublings and repetitions of the play... if the first was mere game, so may the second be."

36

are really about. Everything predicts her independence from the home cradle – the recoil from the "bitter" drug; the precocious standing alone; the infantile running and waddling; her parents' absence in Mantua; the "fall" foreshadowing future experience; the "earthquake" that heralded her weaning; the "jest" that shall infallibly come true. Her back-story, given here, suggests that she has always been attended by forces beyond the domestic; that she has long been moved by a destiny that her carers observed but could never understand. The real theme of the Nurse's tale, then, is not Juliet's nursing, or her dependence, or even her over-cosseted charm. It is the inevitability of her leaving.

Why is Mercutio so important?

But still we haven't truly found Juliet. And we cannot do so until we meet someone dangerous and new, someone who, I want to suggest, is more crucial even than Romeo in supplying the heroine with her energies. This is Mercutio – the Prince's kinsman, Romeo's friend, and the greatest scene-stealer in Shakespeare.

According to Dryden, Shakespeare had to kill off Mercutio because, if he had not, Mercutio would have killed him. His wit is spellbinding, his motives unspeakable, his mind and tongue so quick that any fellow-feeling for others, or settling in an emotion or a relationship, are made to seem almost retarded. In a sense, he was the most potentially destructive character Shakespeare ever created. Mercutio had to die, or not only this romantic tragedy, but Shakespeare's own career as a sympathetic dramatist, might have been killed by a wit so cold and brilliant.

Mercutio enters the play as the young Montague men head for the Capulet feast. But from the start he is at a curious angle from the rest of the action. He was not involved in the brawl and has no perspective on the city or its tensions. He is of neither family. He hasn't the slightest political interest. He is utterly detached from love. We never see him alone. He never meets Juliet, never learns of Romeo's love for her, and indeed never speaks of her existence. He talks a lot, but always in puns and usually in a way that flies far beyond the understanding and perhaps patience of his hearers. Why is he here?

For many readers and spectators, it seems, Mercutio is here simply to amuse and then to be killed. It is a critical commonplace that *Romeo and Juliet* turns upon his semi-accidental stabbing halfway through: in Coleridge's words, "on the Death of Mercutio the catastrophe depended, and it was produced by it; it served to show how indifference and aversion to activity in Romeo may be overcome, and roused by any deep feeling that is called forth to the most determined actions".

It is the pivotal act for the plot, leading in swift succession to Tybalt's death, Romeo's exile, and the impossibility of the lovers' peaceful marriage. The doom is now publicly upon them. Mercutio's death thus heralds the play's decisive turn to tragedy. Put this way it can sound as though Mercutio is merely a formal counter in the plot. Any friend of Romeo would do; anything to set off the terrible chain reaction. Or, if this is to underplay Mercutio's singular charms, then he is significant mainly in terms of the play's dominant mood. For as long as he is around, the mood is light, and the social world of Verona holds sway. Once he has gone, the lights go out, and the world takes on the form, increasingly dark and macabre, of the lovers' desires. So we leave the streets of Verona, and enter the heady world of violent fancy, night-time congress, morbid dreams, deathlike sleep, and living tombs.

But Mercutio is a far more pregnant figure – he is far more pregnant with the play-world – than this summary allows. This is so for two main reasons. First, it is Mercutio who sets up this world's literally dangerous understanding of language and sex, its uniquely intimate feeling for heady minds and secret turbulence and explosive privacy. Second, it is Mercutio who gives vent and breath to the passions – passions that for all his compulsive chatter with his friends cannot possibly be socialised – that it is Juliet's purpose to embody, channel, and canonise.

It is immediately clear that Mercutio poses a powerful obstacle to the central story. Both the Montague and Capulet parents are weak and stupid and easily overcome next to him. He dominates Romeo's young male world. He is higher in class, independent of family, geographically mobile, conversationally fearless. In some ways he leads Romeo and his friends; in others, he feeds off them; more profoundly, he wants to pre-empt their going off and doing what young boys will do with young girls: "If love be blind, love cannot hit the mark". (2.1) But he is also almost supernaturally electrified. His wit is perhaps the most pathological that Shakespeare ever scripted. He cannot help it or, it sometimes seems, even control it:

> *Sure wit, follow me this jest, now till thou hast worn out thy pump, that when the single sole of it is worn, the jest may remain after the wearing solely singular. [2.4]*

As he aptly says of himself: "if our wits run the Wild-Goose chase, I am done." (2.4) His wit truly is demonic, in the sense of a passion that possesses him. Equally, his wit is obsessive, returning again and again to sex as its subject, and sex of a very particular kind: aggressive, lonely, violating, degrading ("Prick love for pricking and you beat love down"; "this driveling love is like a great natural that runs lolling up and down to hide his bauble in a hole" (2.4)), redeemed only if tales about it can be traded for laughter with his friends: "O Romeo, that she were, O that she were/ An open-arse and thou a poperin pear" (2.2, in which the repeated "O" signifies sexual groaning and the "O" of the vagina). His is the negative sublime, turning awe and obsession into ridicule. It is not Rosaline who is Juliet's true rival – it is Mercutio.

From the start Mercutio can be understood to exist in a kind of rival play, a virtual thing that grows out of his witticisms. The best example of this is his famous speech about the Queen of the Fairies, Mab. It is a classically Shakespearean construction, with conceits and fables tumbling one out of another. In this speech Mercutio supplies a rival version of love, creation, and the comic-tragic; a rival aesthetic to both Romeo's borrowed lyricism and Juliet's lucidity and directness; and a rival idea of how the world can be made and remade simply in the eyes of a lover. It is essentially a tale of genesis, tracing the spirit of desire and inception:

She is the fairies' midwife, and she comes
In shape no bigger than an agate stone
On the forefinger of an alderman,
Drawn with a team of little atomi

Over men's noses as they lie asleep.
Her chariot is an empty hazelnut
Made by the joiner squirrel or old grub,
Time out o' mind the fairies' coachmakers;
Her waggon-spokes made of long spinners' legs,
The cover of the wings of grasshoppers,
Her traces of the smallest spider web,
Her collars of the moonshine's watery beams,
Her whip of cricket's bone, the lash of film,
Her waggoner a small grey-coated gnat,
Not half so big as a round little worm
Prick'd from the lazy finger of a maid;
And in this state she gallops night by night
Through lovers' brains, and then they dream of
love; [1.4}

The vision is most obviously childlike: in its anthropomorphising of vegetable and insect life, and in its magnifying quickening of a natural world usually thought too small to describe or too static to command interest. In this it is like an early Disney cartoon, zooming into an ant's nest or a cricket's body and finding a microcosm of comic possibilities. There is a fantastic power here, an improvisatory creativity just beyond the grasp of customary adult sensation. We might then understand Mercutio as being somehow infantile, sustaining a tight connection to childhood fancy and to a child's casual violence, as though in revenge upon dozy and disappointing maturity. In this the speech prepares us subliminally for the play's true child, Juliet.

But the speech, for all its childlike imaginative brilliance, is also one of escalating violence. What begins as an image of diminutive charm soon turns into an anatomised or brutalised body. Magnification becomes evisceration, promising nothing but a skeleton; or else he envisions nature as a rapidly enveloping web, as cells divide and sub-divide and conquer by various kinds of evacuation, or atrophy, or dismembering: wagon spokes made of long spinners' legs, a cover from the wings of grasshoppers, a whip from the bones of crickets. It is little wonder that this torturous dream-vision soon mutates into an obscurely paranoid nightmare:

Sometime she driveth o'er a soldier's neck
And then dreams he of cutting foreign throats,
Of breachers, ambuscados, Spanish blades,
Of health's five fathom deep; and then anon
Drums in his ear, at which he starts and wakes,
And being thus frighted swears a prayer or two
And sleeps again. [1.4]

Of course Mercutio is still busy enacting his show; it is a nice joke that the soldier should "swear" a prayer. But there is a real feeling of peril here, as though Mercutio has inadvertently lifted the hatch upon his secret terrors – a fear shown at this point in Zeffirelli's film by Mercutio's sudden and alarming distance from his friends. The rising menace, and the clear intimacy of the "soldier" to the speaker, shows the dream-vision moving closer and closer to wakefulness. The volatility ceases to be that of dream and becomes that of half-waking: and so of an adulthood anxious to slide away from memory and accountability and back into intoxication.

Ultimately, Mercutio's endlessly unfolding conceit wants to wither down both significance and experience. Pretending merely to offer an entertainment to his friends, he reveals a peculiarly lonely and even sadistic psychopathology, in which super-soldering wit burns itself up into cold and wintry exile. (It is suggestive here that the sole hint of Mercutio's nature in Shakespeare's source was that he had "cold hands"). Mercutio tries to construct his own rival cosmos, free from the "pricks" and disappointments of flesh – a parallel dimension in which metaphoric language takes the place of bodies, action, and motive. But his fantasy eventually turns into exactly what he would escape – misogyny and physical disgust, the invisible seeds of life turned ugly and malevolent:

> *That is that very Mab*
> *That plaits the manes of horses in the night*
> *And bakes the elf-locks in foul sluttish hairs,*

Opposite: Queen Mab, *Gustave Doré, (1832-1883)*

Which, once untangled, much misfortune bodes.
This is the hag, when maids lie on their backs,
That presses them and learns them first to bear,
Making them women of good carriage. [1.4]

The fairy tale "wagon" with which the speech
began has mutated into the "good carriage"
of unwanted pregnancy, just as Mab has
metamorphosed into a devilish succubus.
Mercutio's vision also clearly recalls the Nurse's
husband's "jest" about Juliet falling "backward"
– that is, having sex – when she has "more wit":
here, in Mercutio's dystopian scene of genesis, is
the "more wit" that this earlier scene predicted.
The point to grasp is that Mercutio, through sheer
imaginative force, has become a rival nurse, and
even "midwife", to the tragic tale of the heroine.

One sign of this is that his vision carries clear
maledictory force. As the critic Joseph A. Porter
says, there is "an effect of clairvoyance" in
everything Mercutio says and does; his visions and
curses work telepathically, and live beyond him in
others. Romeo begs him "peace, peace", Benvolio
complains that his words "blow us from ourselves",
as though both are afraid of falling into the self-
same vortex as their friend. And they are half-right
– but Romeo is not being blown from himself but
strangely into himself, the vortex being the world
of Mercutio's fantasy, threatening to come
surreally true. Consequently, the speech generates

a kind of magical causal energy, half-blessing, half-cursing all action performed in its wake. The moment Mercutio stops speaking, Romeo confesses that his "mind misgives" that the "night revels" to which Mercutio is leading him shall "expire the term of a despised life". Already – mercurially, as Mercutio's name suggests – Queen Mab is at work, the midwife of violence, turning desire into death.

How does Mercutio prepare us for Juliet?

It is a basic purpose of Mercutio at once to dazzle us and tire us out, to seem to take us far from home or from our comforts, and to make us long for something simple, plaintive, and true, something we think we already know: and this known thing, of course, is true love. Shakespeare absolutely understands these feelings. He orchestrates and satisfies them, as Mercutio's hurly-burly garrulousness makes way for the silent, gazed-upon wonder of Juliet. However, the difference between them is only part of the story.

Of course it is the violent contrast between Mercutio and Juliet that will most immediately strike home – especially as this contrast plays with Romeo, in terms of competing claims upon the hero's attention. Here Mercutio has no chance.

The freshness of Juliet's beauty suggests an incommensurably different creation from that of Mab, just as Mercutio's crabbed and prevented homo-eroticism cannot compete with the fully possessed, full-frontal sensuousness of Juliet.

That Mercutio is relatively so crippled – suffering the simple impossibility of satisfied or even fully articulated desire – is his personal tragedy. But as much as Juliet is Mercutio's opposite, replacing sexual repulsion with delight, she is no less of a death-dealer than Mab. If Mercutio is Juliet's rival, she is also his inheritor. Once he dies, his astonishing diabolical energy is passed as though by osmosis into her. He is killed, in a very basic sense, for her. But what we need to see is that this osmosis is already at work in the Queen Mab speech – not least because, among many things, it also enacts a rehearsal or premonition of Mercutio's killing, struck down in full hyper-comic flow:

MERCUTIO
   This is the hag, when maids lie on their backs,
   That presses them, and learns them first to bear,
   Making them women of good carriage:
   This is she –
ROMEO
                      Peace, peace, Mercutio, peace.
   Thou talk'st of nothing. [1.4]

Romeo's interruption is indeed a kind of dagger, sending his friend precipitously into "peace". And as such, it symbolically achieves exactly what his actual death does a few scenes later – Mab's "good carriage" gives vent to Juliet: "This is she." In the telepathic logic of Shakespeare's creation, "she" is precisely the "nothing" of which Mercutio speaks: "nothing" in the sense of a woman (the irresistible vagina-joke made various times in the play); "nothing" in the sense that this imminent fairy queen has not yet come to be.

There is nothing haphazard about what Shakespeare is crafting here. He is gestating Juliet, almost giving birth to her, all the time that Mercutio spins his fantastical web. He miniaturises what the play expands into tragedy. For as we shall see, there are compelling subterranean affinities between the rival fairy queens, Mab and Juliet: they both redeem clichés and render creation newly vital, swarming with unconsidered possibilities; they both make words and passions come alive, as though for the very first time.

Furthermore, the two fairy queens share in the driven remorselessness of their vocations, as revealed in the action of the speeches and stories that render them: both pledged to the pitilessness of desire, and to the fact that it takes no prisoners on the path to satisfaction; both aware of how the coming alive of dreams is necessarily a coming into mortality, into flesh as the end, in all senses, of sex.

Juliet's private passions repeatedly imagine dissevered bodies and ghastly death-in-life unions, ultimately played out in a ghastly tomb. And yet it is not the macabre or even the fleshly that is the final resting place of their companionship. Both of them, Mab and Juliet, inhabit some space beyond the mortal, so that all of their actions, as seen in flesh, seem to be only traces of a far truer metaphysical domain, of which their visible lives can give only tantalising witness and promise. There are worlds elsewhere.

Queen Mab showcases the terrors and charisma of a truly Shakespearean imagination. This is why the speech is so celebrated, and why it is never cut in performance: it is difficult to know the speech's purpose in the story or relevance to the speaker, but it is always clear that it is a masterpiece of creative improvisation. We seem to be listening in to creation at its source, or to be seeing it anew, like a god might, each secret constituent magnified and weirdly manifest. This is the supercharged mind that creates worlds like *Romeo and Juliet* – a mind and a vision that cannot rest in what is merely apparent; that cannot help seeing what lies beneath; that cannot resist looking so closely at beauty that it begins to look like horror. Mercutio's x-ray vision is the play's.

Why is Romeo's first glimpse of Juliet so important?

The idea of Juliet as a kind of time-traveler, or delicate alien, is repeated when Romeo first lays eyes upon her: "What lady is that which doth enrich the hand/Of yonder Knight?" Romeo's response is characteristically ardent, lyrical, and conceit-ridden, but there is a change from the narcissistic pseudo-paradoxes of before. His language has suddenly fastened upon a subject of both recognition and wonder:

> *O, she doth teach the torches to burn bright.*
> *It seems she hangs upon the cheek of night*
> *As a rich jewel in an Ethiop's ear –*
> *Beauty too rich for use, for earth too dear [1.5]*

The terms of praise that Romeo uses are now intimately keyed in to Shakespeare's deeper purposes. This un-named lady teaches the "Torches to burn bright". Most immediately this invokes the torches at the night-mask. She gives the event, designed to identify and rank beauty, its model to imitate. The torches are also bearers or symbols of desire, the hopeful fire that carries the masquers through the evening. But Juliet does more than light the sensual flame. The secret is in

Shakespeare's alliterations. She teaches, and the teaching becomes a torch; she torches, and in that teaches. Similarly, she burns, and the burning is bright; she is bright, and the brightness burns. We can feel her heat, at source, as the alliteration discharges a physical transference that works like touch, or even impregnation. The words produce each other in such a way that everything is at once a noun, an adjective, and a verb: in other words, a quality moving with life.

The conceits that herald Juliet never simply dress her, in the way of language as ornament. They never simply compare her to some already-known superlative. They produce her, and she produces them: "It seems she hangs upon the cheek of night,/As a rich Jewel in an Ethiop's ear". We sense immediately that Romeo is the first truly to recognise her – as being from elsewhere, as not being home, as far from the habitual as is imaginable.

This is suggested by the exotic Ethiop, but more subtly by Romeo's curious placing of her. For it is telling that this hanging upon the "cheek of night" completes a couplet: "O she doth teach the torches to burn bright:/It seems she hangs upon the cheek of night". The "Ethiop's ear" only comes in at the end of the next line, contributing to a quite different couplet. The image we remember is this one: "she hangs upon the cheek of night". In this image she does not hang "from" anything (like an

SIX KEY QUOTES

"*What's in a name? that which we call a rose*
By any other word would smell as sweet."

Juliet [2.2]

"*O, she doth teach the torches to burn bright.*
It seems she hangs upon the cheek of night
As a rich jewel in an Ethiop's ear –
Beauty too rich for use, for earth too dear!"

Romeo [1.5]

"*He jests at scars that never felt a wound.*
But, soft, what light through yonder window breaks?
It is the east and Juliet is the sun."

Romeo [2.2]

"*O Romeo, Romeo, wherefore art thou Romeo?*
Deny thy father and refuse thy name.
Or, if thou wilt not, be but sworn my love,
And I'll no longer be a Capulet"

Juliet [2.2]

"*A plague o' both your houses!*"

Mercutio [3.1]

"*Give me my Romeo; and when I shall die*
Take him and cut him out in little stars.
And he will make the face of heaven so fine
That all the world will be in love with night,
And pay no worship to the garish sun."

Juliet [3.2]

ear), but "upon" the cheek. She defies gravity, magically suspended; there is no source for the hanging, or none but herself. She is self-sufficient, a mini-world in herself. But Juliet makes worlds as much as embodies them.

Words here are not so much describing as ushering possibilities into motion. As the torch that burns bright, Juliet precedes even the sun; as the sole bright white pearl on the cheek of night, she makes the sunless sky her own. In either case, without her – before or after her – there is absolute darkness. This makes Juliet far more than a primal flame, more than a source of life or a model of beauty. For if torches is Juliet's personal verb as well as an objective noun – she *torches* – then it reinforces the literally consummating suggestion of "burn". Such radiance cannot last; it is premised on expiring. She will end, but so will the world of which she is the animating spirit. When she is gone – and it is already certain she will go – the world will be dull, grey, passionless, lukewarm, even as it survives into the bone-coloured day.

Romeo's praise establishes the first principles of Juliet's presence. She is more autochthonous (of earth and origins) than anyone else in the play, because more intimately conspiring with the matter that exists before names and orders. But if she is this matter – kinetic, flushed through with energy – she will necessarily only be a kind of visitor to anyone else's world, the punctual world with its names and institutions. In other words, she is essentially at odds with the clocks. Her time is no one else's. When she enters into passion – her love for Romeo, the torch burning bright – she simply re-makes night or day as her own property. And if the premise is absolute, so must be the consequences. She has to burn up, because the given world cannot accommodate her. But as much as she will pass from these houses, she will not finally pass away, because she must return to where she has come from – the world of original energy. This is a crucial source of the play's remarkable imaginative afterlife.

What is it that makes the balcony scene so memorable?

The scene on the balcony is the most celebrated in the play – perhaps the most famous scene in all of drama. It grabbed the attention from the very start. The vogue for *Romeo and Juliet* was clearly at its height in the last years of the century, leading to the rash of parodies and/or tributes in 1600-01 such as in Ben Jonson's *Poetaster* (1601) and Marston's *The Insatiate Countess* (performed in 1610 but probably first scripted ten years earlier). The parodies tell us much about *Romeo and*

Juliet's reception and repetition, repeatedly exaggerating the same few things. But what of the original?

The balcony scene begins with a soliloquy from Romeo. The speech is amusing and intimate, as Romeo, unseen by anyone but ourselves, watches Juliet emerge from her upper window. Whereas before Shakespeare was giving Romeo's words a depth-charge which exceeded the speaker's simple purpose of praise, here Romeo speaks with the careful, explicatory detail of clear intention: "It is the East, and Juliet is the Sun,/Arise fair Sun and kill the envious Moon..." Of course his metaphors of sun, moon, and heaven are conventional – but they escape convention, or rather validate it, precisely because they are a coming-true of what we have already glimpsed and treasured:

> *Two of the fairest stars in all the heaven,*
> *Having some business, do entreat her eyes*
> *To twinkle in their spheres till they return.*
> *What is her eyes were there, they in her head?*
> *The brightness of her cheek would shame those*
> *   stars*
> *As daylight doth a lamp. Her eyes in heaven*
> *Would through the airy region stream so bright*
> *That birds would sing and think it were not*
> *   night. [2.2]*

But the speech is at the same time kept honest

by Romeo's attention to simple physical presence – Juliet's body so close, her shining eyes, the voice about to speak, and above all her "cheek", already hanging in the play's air as the mysterious epitome of beauty. The tension comes from her proximity. That she may overhear him as he can overhear her; that she may see him as he sees her; that she hasn't yet done so, but he and we wish she would, though perhaps not quite yet... The tension is exquisite and, inevitably, erotic.

It is suggestive that "cheek" is Juliet's cue-word, and that it is spoken twice earlier in the speech – inviting Juliet to enter early with repeated sighs of "Ay me". This reinforces the most obvious effect of the speech, which is to suspend us in desire to hear Juliet properly speak, as herself, free from the barriers that so far have inhibited her (with Nurse and Mother, obviously) but also in her first surprised meeting with Romeo, when she was forced to hide behind the masked charade of "Pilgrims' hands" and Saints' prayers.

And now, at last, Juliet truly speaks. It is no accident that this moment also heralds the most famous line in the play: "O Romeo, Romeo, wherefore art thou Romeo?" This is the first full line spoken by Juliet to herself. The line can be hard to think about because it is so well-known. But it does contain a puzzle or two. The line is often misheard or misinterpreted, so as to mean where is Romeo? (rather than why or with what dire consequences he is named Romeo). There may be some performative explanations for this – it is likely that an actor will stress the first syllable, "where", perhaps swallowing or eliding "fore". Either way it is likely that Shakespeare recognised the potential ambiguity; he might have written "why" instead of "wherefore". However, he doesn't, and this allows us legitimately to infer the question we feel sure she is thinking, even if it is concealed in a different question: where art thou, Romeo?

THE BALCONY SCENE

In the years after *Romeo and Juliet* the popular stage witnessed a series of parodies of the balcony scene, a sure sign of instant fame. Henry Porter's *Two Angry Women of Abingdon* (1598) and Thomas Dekker's Blurt, *Master Constable* (1607) both replace the scene's already-famous love lyricism with frank bawdy punning; John Marston's *Jack Drum's Entertainment* (1600) mockingly sugars the language of ardour to saccharine excess. And of course the tradition has gone on. But what was it that seems to have made the scene so immediately iconic? These days, the scene is mainly celebrated as one of simple, ardent, young love, precious partly as a kind of primal romantic scene (spawning a million imitations), partly as a fresh, as yet un-disappointed expression of hope, truth, faith, and delight. This alone, perhaps, is easily mocked, especially by the disappointed or – much the

The simple visual irony of the scene certainly begs the question. After all, Romeo is right there, but she doesn't know it, and already we assume that she longs, as he does, for the beloved's human presence.

The second puzzle is that Juliet bemoans his Christian name rather than what by rights she should be cursing, which is the surname he shares with the rest of the Montagues. But the explanation is clear: "Romeo" is so much more

---

same thing – the satiric intelligence.

Ben Jonson's parody of the balcony scene in *Poetaster* (1601) is a case in point. The Emperor Augustus's daughter, Julia, enters "above" at her chamber window and calls out "Ovid? My love?", to which he replies, in a stock romantic conceit, "Here, heavenly Julia". Immediately Julia begins quibbling over their situation: "Here? And not here? Oh, how that word doth play/With both our fortunes, differing like ourselves;/Both one, and yet divided, as opposed:/I high, thou low", and so on

(4.10. 1-8).

Jonson's parody is rooted in distaste for cliché. Here she is, another besotted lover, on another balcony, and how inconvenient that, yet again, the absence of a staircase should so frustrate the course of true love! Jonson is also getting a hit in against Shakespeare's Juliet. Who quibbles over words in a love scene, as Juliet does with her "rose is a rose". Shakespeare simply cannot keep to decorum! Jonson's parody makes the whole balcony scene absurd and tasteless – witness Julia's desperate imprecation to "enjoy me amply still". ◆

intimate to Juliet than "Montague" could ever be. The sound of his name is beautiful to her, the more so in English with its adjacent sighs (oh) separated only by the personal pronoun (me). The relatively tinny and adult "Montague" could not remotely perform this function. As it is, Ro-me-o, thrice-spoken, gathers a charge of eroticised wordplay (preparing for her ecstatic punning on the wedding night). The result is that one sense – her ostensible rejection of the name – is subverted by another: her powerful feeling for the name.

For "Romeo", as the title declares and everyone already knows, is the only name that belongs with "Juliet". Indeed Juliet almost conjures with the name here, as though calling upon his spirit to appear by the simple charm or incantation of her repetitions. Here as elsewhere, Shakespeare gives to Juliet the prestige of making things come true. So, her conjuring with Romeo's name follows immediately upon Mercutio's mock conjuring, immediately before this scene, of the "wrong" mistress, Rosaline ("I conjure thee by Rosaline's bright eyes... Scarlet lip... Quivering thigh,/And the Demeanes, that there Adjacent lie"), which itself followed hard upon Benvolio's desperate call for "Romeo, my Cozen Romeo, Romeo". Shakespeare is setting up symmetrical or answering scenes, as he often does in this play, whereby a false call (or name, or praise, or lament) is succeeded by the true one. Understood in this simple scenic sense,

Juliet's is an answering call for Romeo – answering Romeo's desire, our desire, and the now-redundant desires of Romeo's friends.

The conversation that follows is remarkable for how it is at once a miracle of hearts meeting, and almost completely dictated, in its ebbs and spurts, by Juliet. Romeo's speeches are all in essentials identical. He is in love, carried by it as though by an ideal made manifest; all of the world, in his eyes, shall collude in this love, and so he indiscriminately harnesses metaphors from the world's abundance as vows or vehicles of his passion. There is no doubt or mystery in the cues the actor gets, no questions left hanging in the cues he gives Juliet. His target is there to be aimed at, and aim he does.

Juliet is written very differently. She keeps shifting register – speaking very plainly and insisting on plainness in return; risking all with sudden confessions; moving unpredictably and often ambiguously between self-address and direct address to Romeo; leaping into rapturous exclamations which, achieved with difficulty, follow upon the convolutions of her nervous fear ("fain would I dwell on form, fain, fain, deny/What I have spoke... Or if thou thinkest I am too quickly won..."). When she first speaks unguardedly, Juliet's language is strikingly simple. She wants to start from the ground up, from the evidence of what is before her, free from the tyranny of any kind of "proper" nouns:

'Tis but thy name that is my enemy:
Thou art thyself, though not a Montague.
What's Montague? It is nor hand nor foot
Nor arm nor face nor any other part
Belonging to a man. [2.2]

Juliet's words are very close to her, intimate to her emergent sensuality: "My ears have yet not drunk a hundred words/Of thy tongues uttering, yet I know the sound". In emphasising the sound and not the meaning, she returns to the passion with which, apparently contrary to semantics, she repeated her Romeo's name, so clearly relishing the feel of the sounds in her mouth. Likewise, the sensory confusion here (ears drinking) is not so much malapropism as a kind of category-eluding synaesthesia. All her senses blend into a single excitement. This is consistent with her basic purpose in the play, to see through, or exist before, the divisions which artificially separate experience from enjoyment.

Her speech gathers a joyful, foundational irresistibility that Romeo's more habitual rhapsodies never quite achieve:

But to be frank and give it thee again;
And yet I wish but for the thing I have.
My bounty is as boundless as the sea,
My love as deep: the more I give to thee
The more I have, for are infinite [2.2]

T.S. Eliot, hearing the balcony exchange as a textured musical pattern, calls this "the dominant phrase of the whole duet", as though its central "theme" is sung for the first time pure and entire. And certainly at such moments her speech can seem astonishingly simple, not borrowed at all, despite its unoriginality. It is original in a more profound sense.

Jacques Derrida writes of the "terrible lucidity of Juliet" and it is almost always she who has the truest words for the occasion:

> *I have no joy of this contract tonight:*
> *It is too rash, too unadvis'd, too sudden,*
> *Too like the lightning, which doth cease to be*
> *Ere one can say 'It lightens'. [2.2]*

Eliot calls "lightning" the play's "key-word", because "significant of the sudden and disastrous power of her passion". But the significance is more than this. This passion is indeed "too like" the lightning. She is left in or as the lightning, *and* in the portentous darkness that succeeds it, waiting for the crash, *and* in the condition of beholding an astonishing experience, outside it as much as in it.

Partly, of course, Juliet's prescient simile anticipates how short-lived this "contract" will be, over almost before it has begun. But she is also acknowledging a passion that makes her consciously feel her inability to muster the words

TEN FACTS
ABOUT *ROMEO AND JULIET*

1.

At least 20 operas have been based on *Romeo and Juliet*. The earliest is Georg Benda's *Roméo und Julie* (1776), and the best-known Gounod's *Roméo et Juliette*. Berlioz's *Romeo et Juliette*, a "symphonie dramatique" for mixed voices, chorus and orchestra, premiered in 1839. Tchaikovsky's *Romeo and Juliet Fantasy-Overture*, a long symphonic poem, has the best known theme. The most famous ballet is by Prokofiev. It was commissioned by the Kirov Ballet, but it was rejected by them, first because Prokofiev attempted a happy ending, and then because the music was too experimental.

2.

Romeo and Juliet is one of the first Shakespeare plays to have been performed outside England: a shortened, simplified version was performed in the Bavarian town of Nördlingen in 1604. Later, Goethe's version of 1811 would hold the Berlin stage until 1849. Unusually, he cut Queen Mab; more prophetically, he also cut the final reconciliation.

3.

A Midsummer Night's Dream, also written around 1595, may parody *Romeo and Juliet* in the entertainment performed by Bottom and friends before the court. In this burlesque interlude, the young lovers, Pyramus and Thisbe, are separated by a "vile wall". They attempt to elope, but Pyramus, mistakenly thinking Thisbe has been killed, commits suicide, whereupon Thisbe stabs herself in despair: "This is the silliest stuff I ever heard," declares Hippolyta.

4.

Romeo and Juliet has been filmed more than any other Shakespeare play except *Hamlet*, and in more languages – 61 times since 1900. The earliest film (1902) was followed by a number of other silent films including one from Italy (1911), the first to use Veronese locations.

5.

Franco Zeffirelli's 1968 film starred a 15-year-old Olivia Hussey as Juliet. Zeffirelli had to get special permission from the Italian censors for Hussey to appear in the nude wedding night scene. She wasn't legally able to attend the London premiere of the film because she was under 18 and the film contained a nude scene.

6.

There is a municipal organization in Verona dedicated to replying to the thousands of love-struck correspondents who write each year to "Juliet" asking for her blessing.

7.

The play has inspired much popular music, including Elvis Costello's *Mystery Dance, The Juliet Letters*, Dire Straits' *Romeo and Juliet* and *Romeo had Juliette*, from Lou Reed's 1989 album *New York*, as well as tracks by The Supremes, Bruce Springsteen, Tom Waits and Radiohead. The play also inspired Leonard Bernstein and Stephen Sondheim's *West Side Story*, set in mid-1950s New York between the feuding Puerto-Rican "Sharks" and white working-class "Jets".

8.

In 1593 the Privy Council closed all London theatres, initially because of a riot, then because there was an outbreak of the plague. The theatres remained closed until 1594. The critic Jonathan Bate notes how plague is subtly woven into the plot of *Romeo and Juliet* – it is because Friar John is detained for fear that he might have been infected that Romeo doesn't receive Friar Laurence's crucial letter.

9.

As with all Shakespeare's plays, *Romeo and Juliet* has been repeatedly adapted and changed to suit contemporary tastes. The prime example of this is David Garrick's great 18th-century adaptation. First performed in 1748, it held the stage for nearly a century. Garrick trimmed comic passages, and removed bawdy ones. Juliet wakes before Romeo is dead, and Garrick added 75 lines of pathetic dialogue after Romeo takes the poison. In 1750, due to audience demand, he also cut all references to Rosaline, as a blemish on Romeo's character – heroes should be ideally noble.

10.

Suicide occurs an unlucky 13 times in Shakespeare's plays. It occurs in *Romeo and Juliet* where both Romeo and Juliet commit suicide, in *Julius Caesar* where both Cassius and Brutus die by consensual stabbing, as well as Brutus' wife Portia, in *Othello* where Othello stabs himself, in *Hamlet* where Ophelia is said to have "drowned" in suspicious circumstances, in *Macbeth* when Lady Macbeth dies, and finally in *Antony and Cleopatra* where suicide occurs an astounding five times (Mark Antony, Cleopatra, Charmian, Iras and Eros).

that might control it or credit it: "ere one can say, it lightens". The simple descriptive phrase, "it lightens", is belated, inadequate, somehow tiny and irrelevant. The event has already happened; words come limping meekly after.

The new world that she has entered is far too vivid and particular for such (approximate) denotations: "it lightens" is a tired generalisation, far removed from life-giving passion. Again we can see how Juliet's true language never simply describes things. Description assumes that the thing described is separate from the language being used, or from the passion that attends its experiencing. Description escapes experience; it puts it to rest, leaves it behind, accommodates itself without struggle to evolving eventualities: it lightens. Such phrases flatten and generalize experience, allowing for livable continuity. Merely to be able to say "it lightens" is the impossible antithesis of Juliet's situation. There would be relief in such words; they would signify survival, a light ahead, a light-ening of terror. But this is not Juliet's experience. Lightning, for her, is not alleviation. It is the sudden irrevocability of that thing, lightning, which she and her lover have become – and it is the stunned, silent darkness that succeeds it.

A scene from the 1961 film West Side Story. *Leonard Bernstein's musical, set in 1950s' New York, was inspired by* Romeo and Juliet *(see page 66)*

What's in a name?

Names – and the significance attached to names – are very important in *Romeo and Juliet*. This is clear from certain names that Shakespeare invents – "Mercutio", for example, inevitably suggests mercurial, which is the perfect adjective for that character's dazzling unpredictability, his quicksilver volatility.

But it is the eponymous couple whose names matter most. It is an easy point to miss, but the title itself – the play's name – encapsulates their tragedy. It is not named Capulet and Montague.

It is not called this, we might want to say, because those are not their names. They are Romeo and Juliet! They are not to be bound up in those patriarchal surnames, surnames which (fail to) distinguish any number of Verona's wealthy rabble. The young lovers are unique, they are individuals, they demand Christian names alone. It is precisely their dissevering of name and identity from the dead signature of family that makes them what they are. And indeed, even individual Christian names are not really what these lovers achieve. They create a new compound, Romeo-and-Juliet, or Juliet-and-Romeo, which rings through the city and ages like an integral life-force, an unimpeachable, shared persona.

But of course all of this is only half-true. They are always also Montague and Capulet. These names cannot be disowned, and they follow, shadow, and survive the titular names like an enveloping doom: or if they don't survive them in popular memory, in our world, they most certainly do in the playworld of Verona.

That this play is a drama of naming, a drama about the possibilities and pre-determinations of being named, is clear from the way the couple first meets. As Susan Snyder nicely puts it, they meet "unlabelled", a "faceless youth and an anonymous girl". They are ignorant of each other's name; we are not, and we await the delicious re-writing or de-writing of the family scripts. But if at one level there is everything to play for, at another it is all already written:

ROMEO:
   Is she a Capulet?
   O dear account! My life is my foe's debt...
JULIET:
   My only love sprung from my only hate.
   Too early seen unknown, and known too late![1.5]

Juliet, as ever, pounces upon the true difficulty: that knowing is not simply an attribute of seeing and appraising. It is not open to us to experience someone as though no one has ever been here before us, or to pretend that we can know who they are merely from such witnessing. For this person precedes the meeting, and is already named. The name is like a stamp, or a brand, linking the person backward to a family and forward to a destiny.

Hence the word "character": in Shakespeare's day this didn't principally mean one's nature or personality; it didn't mean a role in a story. It meant writing, the letters themselves. Character is written: it is a name. Our modern understanding of "character" was beginning to emerge (partly through Shakespeare's work). But if Romeo and Juliet contributes powerfully to an ideology of subjective freedom, in which we can forge our own characters, and come to our own conclusions about the characters of others we meet, it also butts up hard against the obstacles to such freedom.

Of course Juliet resists, as she must, the tyranny of this signifier:

> *'Tis but thy name that is my enemy:*
> *Thou art thyself, though not a Montague.*
> *What's Montague? It is nor hand nor foot*
> *Nor arm nor face nor any other part*
> *Belonging to a man. O be some other name.*
> *What's in a name? That which we call a rose*
> *By any other word would smell as sweet... [2.2]*

Juliet is fighting against convention, and against

CUTS, CENSORINGS AND PERFORMANCE VERSIONS

From the very start, it would seem, Shakespeare's full text of *Romeo and Juliet* has almost never been performed. The very first printed version of Shakespeare's play from 1597 is much shorter than the one usually published in modern editions. It includes lots of unique stage directions, and clearly either records or prescribes theatrical performance. Quite where it comes from is much disputed. It may have been abridged from a fuller playtext for the purposes of performance, probably as a touring copy. It may have been a pirated copy, published to exploit the play's obvious popularity. It may have been put together from the memory or notes of people who have witnessed the full play, either in the audience or as actors. But whatever the story behind the text, it gives us a good naming as the acme of such convention, in the cause of sensory and sensual immediacy. And part of this immediacy is a kind of instinctive resistance to proper nouns:

Deny thy father and refuse thy name.
Or if thou wilt not, be but sworn my love
And I'll no longer be a Capulet. [2.2]

"Be but sworn my love": the name she prefers is not primarily a name, although of course she can address him simply as that. "My love" is a feeling, an action. Of course the compounding of verb and

---

insight into how the story was cut to ensure a swift and streamlined performance.

The cuts are mainly of four kinds: one, unnecessary narration/reportage; two, long speeches of piety or poeticizing, particularly from the Friar; three, bawdy punning; four, Juliet's speeches, especially in the second half of the play. Most of these changes can be explained by performance. For example, it may be that a new actor had to take over the part of Juliet, because the adolescent for whom the part had originally been written had grown up too much, or because they were touring. The new actor may have lacked the experience to take on Juliet's more challenging speeches - hence the renewed accent on stage directions to carry the part. More broadly the cuts produce a swiftly economical acting text, getting rid of highly conceited passages, of the kind that perhaps reward reading more than hearing.

Clearly some aspects of the play were from the very start acknowledged to be theatrically unwieldy or indulgent. And every successful version of the play has cut it radically.

The same cuts recur again and again: Romeo's love for Rosaline, his bad poetry, and his murder of Paris; Juliet's erotic wordplay, sexual hunger, and morbid fantasies; lots of Mercutio's puns (though they always include Queen Mab); Benvolio's plot summaries; the Friar's tutorials; the musicians' singing and joking after Juliet's apparent death; the Nurse is sometimes cut sharply (Luhrmann), sometimes expanded as the fallible moral heart of the story (Zeffirelli, *West Side Story*).

The ending is usually changed. For centuries Juliet would wake before Romeo's death, to allow a final exchange between the two. These days the play tends to end very quickly after Juliet's suicide, cutting the Friar's explanations and, often, the fathers' reconciliation.

Some of the cuts are no doubt good ones. But in the main they make the story much less tonally various, much more the expected thing. It becomes a simple story of true love. The lovers lose their wildness and eccentricity, and become basically good and ideal. This is especially true of Romeo. Shakespeare's Romeo is much more satirized than most of his later incarnations, particularly early on, and he is more violent later in the play. Shakespeare's Juliet is much more sexual and death-driven than most subsequent versions allow.

More than anything, the popular versions tend to cut Shakespeare's stylistic variance – his ironies, sudden juxtapositions of style or scene, ironic counterpoints.

Shakespeare's play is more of an ensemble-piece; there are more telepathic connections between characters (eg Mercutio and Juliet); it is much more antic. As Dr Johnson has it: "his pathetic strains are always polluted by some unexpected depravations." Shakespeare's adaptors have long felt it their duty to protect us from the playwright's bad taste.◆

name in one word is another epitome of one of the play's central tragic paradoxes – that the thing we wish to possess can only be possessed in the passing; that to freeze or canonize it is to rob it of life; but that without such naming all we have is loss.

In his essay, "The Murdering World", Kiernan Ryan says that for Juliet and Romeo a "way of life which had seemed unquestionable is exposed as a prison-house, whose walls are built of words". Among the words which make the walls are their names. But the names – their first names, both treasured individually and as a compound – are also stolen from their families and re-possessed passionately as their own. Names brand us as mortal and confined; they also confer immortality.

How does Juliet speak her love?

Juliet is as restless in language as she is in her home – as restless and searching as any of Shakespeare's great originals. It is she who gives the balcony scene its powerful feeling of imminence – of something life-changing about to happen. But she also knows that this imminence depends for its power upon its very real precariousness. Things could go either way – they might be found out, her beloved killed; he might be tricking her, or seducing her merely for immediate "satisfaction" ("I will take thy word, yet if thou swear'st,/Thou mayest prove false"). She is the one who, very directly, declares love in a manner that is not hedged by convention, and who demands an answer from the other ("Dost thou Love?"). She is the one who blasts away, through sheer lucidity of thought and feeling, any carapace of romantic precedent, just as she refuses all the oaths of attachment, as being in hock to discredited convention. She is the one who is repeatedly called back by the umbilical cord of home (the Nurse or Mother's cries) but who repeatedly returns despite it, preferring the "silken thread" of a love that shall "kill" with "much cherishing". She is the one who, returning after confessing her love, cannot but push through to the "marriage" that is indeed her only "honourable" course – again risking the young boy's retreat or even ridicule.

He doesn't retreat, of course – but it is she who makes all the running. It is Juliet who at once alters the given world, apprehends the risks, and pushes through regardless. And Romeo is electrified into his truth by her – galvanized out of borrowed gestures or easy self-gratification.

And what is true here of his language is repeated throughout their story. Each time Romeo is there first (to love, erotic anticipation, self-destructive resolutions, suicide) but in a slightly callow, theatrical way. Juliet takes the stakes into herself

Olivia Hussey and Leonard Whiting in Franco Zeffirelli's 1968 film

absolutely – as she ultimately does the killing knife. In this Juliet establishes the model for many of Shakespeare's women: the heroines of comedy, who always tutor the men in erotic truth, all the way to Cleopatra, who after the fumbling humiliations of Antony's attempts at suicide shows how it really should be done.

If there is a single speech which sums up Juliet, it is perhaps the liberating, violent intensity of this:

Hist! Romeo, hist! O for a falconer's voice
To lure his tassel-gentle back again.
Bondage is hoarse and may not speak aloud,
Else would I tear the cave where Echo lies
And make her airy tongue more hoarse than mine

She is calling for Romeo, wishing herself more powerful, unafraid of transgressing gender roles (a falconer with a bird), impatient of restrictions, bursting to escape the "bondage" of home and language. Juliet is alone here, calling at once for her lover and for a better language, a fuller voice: the two are reciprocal, for she knows how it is the language of their society, in the fullest sense of available communication and interpersonal rules, which inhibits her desire from free expression.

Romeo is briefly absent; she fears he has disappeared; so she imagines, with the full force of her being, herself as the abandoned lover, left to grieve the cruelly departed boy. This is why she inhabits and transforms the archetypal lovelorn figure of Echo, who in Ovid's *Metamorphoses* – Shakespeare's favourite book – wails so much for her lover as to turn, literally, into a bodiless lamenting voice. Juliet's conceit telescopes time and place. It takes her beyond this moment, extending it into a fate and a myth, pushing back into the primal tales of Shakespeare's creative world. Simultaneously she projects ahead into her own future state, when she will herself become a mythical model of the abandoned tragic lover.

But she is not content to repeat Echo's misery – Juliet disdains to be a mere echo. For Juliet, Echo's abandonment to defeat is doubly a "lie" – to "lie" down and wail life and body away is untrue to the flint of passion. Juliet's fierce grief – or rage is perhaps closer to the mark – is absolutely embodied. It garners its energies and its pain precisely from physical tension: she will "tear the cave", make the tongue "hoarse", in a radical assault upon all confining origins, including those of her own feminine body. So, the "cave" here evokes a multiple primal home – Echo's retreat, and so the cave of mythical possibility; the "room" which so far in her life has kept her in bonds; a voicebox or throat; and perhaps a womb. It amounts to a powerful defiance of social prescription. Neither her body nor her mouth will stay demurely closed. This speech, for all that it is vehemently whispered, is in fact a virtual, virtuoso scream. A bracing dare to be challenged, this speech shows Juliet imaginatively throwing caution to the winds. She has flown the roost, irrevocably.

How does Shakespeare handle time in *Romeo and Juliet*?

The Romantic critic William Hazlitt says of the play that it "presents a beautiful *coup d'oeil* of the progress of human life. In thought it occupies years, and embraces the circle of the affections from childhood to old age." However, it does not represent this "progress" sequentially. Instead, *Romeo and Juliet* is always running simultaneously at different speeds. The story hinges on disjunctions of timing – most notoriously, the accidents that lead to the catastrophe: the letter telling Romeo that Juliet is not dead is outpaced by the false report that she is dead; she wakes up after he has taken the fatal poison. The philosopher Jacques Derrida writes this of the lovers:

> They live in turn the death of the other... Both are in mourning – and both watch over the death of the other, attend to the death of the other... They both live, outlive the death of the other.

However, this "anachrony", as Derrida calls it – meaning time at cross-purposes, one time not harmonising with another – is not confined to the lovers' deaths. It is a basic principle of pretty much every scene.

For instance, the sense of time in the balcony scene is delicate and multiple. The lovers' haste and urgency makes their clock faster than anyone else's. But equally the Nurse's and mother's calls from off-stage relate their own urgent fear that temporal boundaries are being breached – young Juliet should be in bed! This is the context of her repeated leaving and returning, the trope of reluctant departure which features so often in the balcony-scene imitations around 1600. But Juliet's returns are not formalised in any way. They are breathless, yearning, dangerous, showing her straining to break from the "Bondage" both of home and daily time.

A further effect is to multiply our sense of the lovers' knowledge of each other, in a sense to extend their experience far beyond the clock-minutes it is lengthened by. Each return comes after a farewell; each "adieu" is a miniature death, like all such partings, a rehearsal of the final one. So each time she comes back on stage she is in a sense resurrected, not so much kissed alive as coming alive to kiss. The effect is miraculous but also incipiently tragic, because we know it is all happening on borrowed time: the clock is ticking, and lovers do not have infinite lives. All of these returns, in the way of this play, are rehearsals for the departure that will define them. However bright the "lightning" of their meeting, the darkness is waiting, irremovable.

The lovers' time is both a vast expanse, measured by recurring cosmic metaphors of star and night, and a fugitive capsule – an eternalised single moment, as enduring as the passion. Juliet in particular is keyed in to this "subjective" time:

> *JULIET:*
>   *What o clock tomorrow shall I send to thee?*
> *ROMEO:*
>   *By the hour of nine.*
> *JULIET:*
>   *I will not fail. 'Tis twenty years till then. [2.2]*

A similar asymmetry between clock-time and her time recurs when, having sent the Nurse to meet with Romeo, Juliet waits impatiently for her return:

> *The clock struck nine when I did send the Nurse,*
> *In half an hour she promis'd to return..*
> *O, she is lame. Love's heralds should be thoughts*
> *Which ten times faster glides than the sun's*
>
>   *beams*
> *Driving back shadows over lowering hills...*
> *Now is the sun upon the highmost hill*
> *Of this day's journey, and from nine till twelve*
> *Is tree long hours, yet she is not come. [2.5]*

Everything is urgent, running against the clock.

The play keeps such things at the forefront of our minds. This is the reason for Capulet's apparently irrelevant fussing over the day of the proposed nuptials. "Adult" measurements are always at odds with "Love's Herald", either retarding (as with the Nurse) or precipitous (as Capulet with the wedding day). And Juliet, very simply, achieves more in the span of a moment than anyone else – her fantastical anticipation is in a sense no less mercurial and swift than Mercutio's fantastical conceits. The Nurse is off busying herself with whatever, just as her parents are fussing and ordering and arranging things, never still. But even if all she does is wait in her room, Juliet lives more lives than the rest put together.

It is all to do with intensity – and here she is far more concentrated than even her lover. Romeo is careful of his servant, has the leisure to indulge in lengthy exchanges of wit with Mercutio and courtliness with the Nurse. He is often absent from the social world (for example during the fracas, or when off with Juliet) but the moment he returns he instantly flows with its rhythms. He remains society's man. This is so even when he tries to intervene in the quarrel, inadvertently helping Tybalt to kill Mercutio, a surviving allegiance to social codes which means he cannot restrain himself from killing Tybalt in return. The tragedy, from this angle, is rooted in Romeo's irresistible socialisation.

Juliet, by contrast, steams alone, staring at the clock, projecting alternative worlds, cutting straight to the kill the moment she is able:

O God she comes. O honey Nurse what news?
Hast thou met with him? Send thy man away.
                                        [2.5]

Intermediaries like the Nurse or the servant are much more to her than delaying nuisances. They are insults to the immediacy of feeling. Whereas it takes either ostentatious self-pity or fateful accidents to make Romeo truly cast himself beyond society, from the moment Juliet commits to love, she is instinctively a rebel:

But old folks, many feighn as they were dead –
Unwieldy, slow, heavy, and pale as lead. [2.5]

As often happens, her words return to bite her, with fatal irony, when she herself feigns death and soon is pale as lead. She will be the victim of all she would reject – but not before she has condemned it, in the name of electric passion, to irrelevance and superannuation.

Hence her marvellously invigorating entrance to the Friar's in the next scene. The Friar has been tutoring Romeo about loving moderately and in good time, wise saws about how the "sweetest honey/Is loathsome in his own deliciousness",

THE
MOST EX:
cellent and lamentable
Tragedie, of Romeo
and *Iuliet*.

Newly corrected, augmented, and
amended :

As it hath bene sundry times publiquely acted, by the
right Honourable the Lord Chamberlaine
his Seruants.

LONDON
Printed by Thomas Creede, for Cuthbert Burby, and are to
be sold at his shop neare the Exchange.
1599.

"too swift arrives as tardy as too slow". On this cue, Juliet enters. She left the previous scene with a brisk "Hie to high Fortune" and it is with the same swiftness that she now enters. The Friar notes her excitement and seeks at once to meld it to his sententious purposes:

> *Here comes the lady. O, so light a foot*
> *Will ne'er wear out the everlasting flint.*
> *A lover may bestride the gossamers*
> *That idles in the wanton summer air*
> *And yet not fall; so light in vanity. [2.6]*

As always in this play, the speech works at different

THE FRIAR

If later theatre gossip is to be believed, it may well be that Shakespeare himself played the Friar. If so, he chose a figure that, for all its apparent moral self-certainty, seems peculiarly prone to attract ambivalent responses. Julian Glover, who played the Friar for the RSC, nicely captures the part's difficulty for modern audiences. At first he thought the Friar "a bumbling, boring old twerp who gets it all wrong and screws up everybody's lives. (When I told the actor Richard Johnson, a fine Romeo in his day, that I was to take the part, he was vehement – 'He's an old bastard, I hate him!')... The last thing we want is a vicar with a very long speech about 'nature'. He also has a dreadfully tiresome speech at the end, when all the registers. So, his description is also a judgement: her tread is light (delicate and swift) but also light ("idle" and "wanton"); she is carefree but also careless; her body's airy summer ease is the opposite of cold everlasting flint; but it will wear away before the flint does.

In terms of the play's tragic destiny, this is all true. But in terms of its emotional compulsion, it deserves to be swept away as life-denying and even grudging. (The Friar's wisdom requires the "fall" that Juliet's summer forestalls.) Of course, the Friar can be played in performance in all sorts of ways – failed moralist, avuncular friend, reluctantly delighted, at odds with his profession, a

audience wants is to go home, in which he tells us in lugubrious detail the story we already know. The man is a complete waste of time, a bland, ineffectual fool who merely acts as a catalyst. He hasn't even got any jokes!" However, once entrusted with the part, his view changed: "a guru-figure – though one intensely practical – he will unblock your drains as soon as your morals; a sort of touchstone of goodness and emotional responsibility, accessible to people of every age, class or political persuasion". At the end, the Friar realises he has tampered unconscionably with natural processes – and he panics. In this there is a clear structural parallel with the Nurse, recommending bigamy, betraying her ward. The Friar's final speech is all for him, to try to repeat and free himself of grief and guilt: "I personally think the play should be re-named something like 'The Tragedy of the Goode Brother'. The children have passed over to a better place – he has to stay and suffer in this one." ◆

leaf in the breeze, a nosy pander – but whatever choices are made here his text occupies a different sense of time and priority to Juliet. He has the long view; she sees only what is before her; he turns everything into small statuettes for our perusal; her thoughts are like the moment, flying beyond capture. So when the Friar invites her to

> *...let rich music's tongue*
> *Unfold the imagin'd happiness that both*
> *Receive in either by this dear encounter. [2.6]*

Juliet's instant rebuke is beautifully deflating of his presumptuousness:

> *Conceit more rich in matter than in words,*
> *Brags of his substance, not of ornament.*
> *They are but beggars that can count their worth.*
> *[2.6]*

She knows – we know – how fervent is her "imagin'd happiness", but it is not something to be rehearsed for an old busybody's delectation. She is instinctively liberating, a rebel for the heart.

The feminist critic and philosopher Julia Kristeva notes "the ambiguous compression of time caused by the immanence of death", and this is epitomised by how Shakespeare contracts their lovemaking to one night, already nearly over. In Brooke's source-tale, the lovers enjoy a few months of surreptitious sex. Shakespeare cuts it to a single night, and this grabbed in the immediate wake of a crime that they both know has already foreshortened everything. The doom is upon them. The lovers are thus at once in the present, and already past it – the act that preceded the nuptial night has already taken Romeo away. As Hazlitt says, Shakespeare "founded the passion of the two lovers not on the pleasures they had experienced, but on all the pleasures they had not experienced" – and we might add, "would not". We only see the lovers in the wake of their night together, and the way we see them says it all. They are "aloft at the window", debating whether the "fearful" birdsong was the lark or the nightingale:

JULIET:
> Wilt thou be gone? It is not yet near day.
> It was the nightingale and not the lark
> That pierc'd the fearful hollow of thine ear.
> Nightly she sings on yond pomegranate tree.
> Believe me, love, it was the nightingale.

ROMEO:
> It was the lark, the herald of the morn,
> No nightingale.   [3.5]

Juliet desperately wants it to be the nightingale, so as to sustain their loving night. Romeo knows that the "envious" and "severing" morning has come. But as much as the passage from nightingale to lark marks the necessity of time, and so of their passing from each other, equally there is no telling which bird it is. The effect is suggestively metaphysical: the birds have joined to become one; each bird has consumed the other. The passing of time, then, is also its erasing, or its distilling into a single moment. And in turn this moment – when the birds "meet" – eternally repeats the act of the lovers' union: as the nightingale (Juliet), and the lark (Romeo), sing and bill and consume one another.

The scene when they wake, therefore, is indeed a wake – a bittersweet ritual of death-marked remembrance. They are recalling what has been, wishing it replayed, but more profoundly preparing for memories of it to come. We thus witness the lovers as already subjects of nostalgia. In this way, the consummation which the whole story seeks – not just sex, of course, but union – is not quite given. We have missed it, or await it. The scenes are structured so that we, like the lovers, feed upon lack, and wish time faster (hurtling toward extinction) or slower (stopping time, and so another form of extinction).

It's not that we need to see the two making love; it's not that we doubt the marriage is consummated; the dawn scene is usually played with them still in bed, more or less languorously post-coital. But this scene, for all its simulation of homely naturalism, is more essentially animated by the birds that they immediately invoke. The lovers are carried by the birds, as by a living metaphor: the song is an echo of their intimacy, but also of their flight from one another. Like everything tuned to their love, it heralds birth and death. Consequently, there is an intimate link between the most lived-in physicality – sensuous restlessness, the avidity of Juliet, the delicacy of touch, their desire to linger – and the impulse to eternalise: if not to erect a monument, then to arrest time, and to possess something in defiance of its impatience. And what we have, of course, is the play

Why is Juliet so young?

The German philosopher Hegel says this of Juliet:

> Juliet cannot otherwise be taken at the beginning than as a quite childlike simple girl... we perceive that she still has no inner consciousness of herself and the world, no movement, no emotion, no wishes; on the contrary, in all naiveté she has peeped into her surroundings in the world, as into a magic lantern show, without learning anything from them or coming to any reflection on them. Suddenly we see the development of the whole strength of this heart, of intrigue, circumspection, power to sacrifice everything and to submit to the harshest treatment; so that now the whole thing

looks like the first blossoming of the whole rose at once, in all its petals and folds, like an infinite outpouring of the inmost genuine basis of the soul, in which previously there was no inner differentiation, formation and development, but which now comes on the scene as an immediate product of an awakened single interest, unbeknown to itself, in its beautiful fullness and force, out of a hitherto self-enclosed spirit. It is a torch lit by a spark, a bud, only now just touched by love, which stands there unexpectedly in full bloom, but the quicker it unfolds, the quicker too does it droop, its petals gone.

I have been writing about Juliet as though she is an independent woman, scrupulous about language, alert to hypocrisy or pretension, self-policing, prudent at first, but once committed, unabashed and adventurous; unafraid of passion, intent upon emotional and existential fullness rather than timidity or evasion – and so on. But she is 13! The age is Shakespeare's invention, specified repeatedly, in a fashion he repeats nowhere else. In all of the earlier versions of the story, Juliet is at least 16, often 18 years old. What does this mean?

How can a 13-year-old be an exemplar of femininity, a pattern for all aspiring subjects? Or is it wrong to think Shakespeare sees her as such? She is 13, a child, and she runs the same gamut of instinctive emotions that any such child might do confronted by the same exciting invitations.

Who wouldn't be awed and delighted by a beautiful older boy, calling you divine and kissing you, and what is more your family's sworn enemy? Who wouldn't be a little scared, worried about the dangers she has so often gone to bed believing (Capulet men prowling the grounds ready to shoot any strangers!)? And then, this wonderful treat once offered, what 13-year-old wouldn't sit impatiently and petulantly curse when boring old adults – the slow fat Nurse, the tedious moralising Friar – get in the way?

And then the hysterics of the wedding night, the wild vacillations between raging grief and desire, the wish that the night should never end and this manboy never leave her bed, leaping at a new trick to further fool her parents, and the ghoulish old wives' graveyard fantasies that follow. What isn't simply childlike – as though her life enjoys the magical facility of making childhood fancies come true?

But this is precisely the problem. The dreams come true, and Juliet remains only 13. What difference does it make to give to a 13-year-old such heat, such ecstatic sexual anticipation, such an awful end, buried alive in a tomb and stabbing herself with a rusty knife? Is it scarier than if she were 18 or 16? In her essay, *"Romeo and Juliet*: The Nurse's Story", Barbara Everett writes this:

The choice of an age slightly young even by

romantic standards achieves the sense of extremity, of a painful "too-soonness"... a sharp recognition of unripeness, of a pathos and gravity recognisably childish, and an acknowledgement that the grief experienced is itself "full, fine, perfect."

This is very eloquent, but does it not beg questions, and in particular make us wonder about the sacrifices required for such "full, fine, perfect" pathos to be achieved?

If we were to hear of such a thing in the real world we would feel, I think, sorrowful and compromised, certain that the poor girl was a victim of delusions or fantasies beyond her station in life. Does the fact that Juliet is in a play license ethical forgetfulness? Isn't it simply creepy to be egging her on, or even to be listening in to a child's sexual fantasies? Shouldn't we feel chastised and guilty? It is bad enough for a young woman to kill herself for love – but a 13-year-old? It is disgusting, obscene; to revel in it, even to imagine it is pornographic! At the very least, shouldn't the fact of her youth make it all simply sadder, with the overwhelming feeling being that she is too young for such emotions or such a fate, that she was mistaken, horribly precocious, that childhood itself has somehow been stolen from her and violated?

But these protests don't quite wash either. Even if her extreme youth makes Juliet blameless, because untutored, then someone, surely, needs to take responsibility for the catastrophe. Her parents, yes, because they want to push her into marriage so young: but then Juliet leaps at the same thing. So do we return to us, or the playwright, or the romantic genre which we and the playwright relish, and which so often likes to sacrifice young women on its altar, as though mere counters in a larger game of "pathos"? We might here compare Juliet, the 13-year-old, to the 14-year-old Marina in Shakespeare's later "romance", *Pericles*: Marina is abducted by pirates for the purposes of gang rape, the scene ends, and next we see her she is being sold as a nice fresh whore to a brothel. What happened in the interim? No one knows; no one asks! Her experience is either impossible – it didn't or couldn't happen! – or else it is ugly and scandalous and deeply shaming to anyone who desires it.

Don't we turn away from Juliet's childishness in the same way? So, she isn't 13, not really: she is a child of romantic tragedy, sculpted for admiration, exemplary sentiments, and ultimately pathos. She remains the generic "heroine", the pastoral princess of hope and possibility, ingenuous symbol of both individuality and community, seen in a hundred plays and a thousand fairy tales and romances.

We might further defend ourselves by admitting that we half turn away from Juliet's age, but that this is not so much an instinct of moral cravenness – forgetting morality in the interests of aesthetic pleasure – as a basic doubleness, an "is and is not", which is typical of Shakespeare. Juliet is and is not 13 – this is a simple fact of how we process her story. One of her distinctive metaphysical "gifts" is that she grows up separate from others, at a different pace or in a subtly different space. This is foreshadowed in numerous ways – for example, the first glimpse we get of her, when her father says she is "yet a stranger in the world"; in her back and forth during the balcony scene, with each exit and re-entrance telescoping vast experiential spaces; the obsessive puns that she speaks, or that rather speak her, suggesting a possession in need of exorcism, stretching her apprehensions way beyond social convention or her experience, beyond even the kinds of sexual rumour that youngsters trade in (as Romeo does early on, for example, with Benvolio and Mercutio). Above all, the changes or decisions that, in "real life", only duration in time allows, are concentrated into single scenes or even speeches of Juliet's, which thereby stand in for their actual doing.

The effect is of accelerated maturation, as though Juliet is the host to possible futures, ones that we never see happening but that are bundled into her as her privilege and burden. She is the heroine who experiences too much, too quickly, on behalf of too many. She is not 13, or 16, or 20: she is simply on the cusp, faced with temptations and forced into decisions that matter. Of course Juliet takes it further. She flies over the cusp. She marries, she has sex, she even dies! Her life is accelerated, as quickly as she wishes time to be for her. She rushes past barriers, into futures. If she enters as a child, she lives into marriage and dies a widow.

But at the same time, hers is the tragedy of never growing up, and of being precipitously cut short before life can truly begin. Who is she to carry a great tragedy, or to speak such astonishing metaphors, or to risk death as she does, not once but repeatedly? All of this engineers a subtle sense that she has been taken over by something, possessed by a force too huge for someone so young. She knows it is all too "sudden" – too quick, too premature – but this "lightning" comes from elsewhere. It is her, in her, but not chosen by her or plotted. This helps furnish the sense of a universal emotion, with Juliet the chosen vessel or the sacrificial lamb. More darkly, it presages the implacability of this world, as she is impelled by something huge and irresistible that carries her beyond all she has known and into death. It is then somehow real and right, and all the more frightening, that Juliet should so intimately imagine consorting with corpses, living as the undead amid the dead. [4.3] In some sense she is always un-dead, always beyond, a refugee from both life and death.

FOUR WAYS CRITICS
HAVE SEEN THE TRAGEDY

1. It was fate. Some critics argue that the lovers are no more than puppets. J.W. Draper says they are literally "star-cross'd" victims, "the puppets of the stars and planets and of the days and times of day".

2. Romantic love is always doomed. Other critics believe, as John Lawlor puts it, that Romeo and Juliet are conquered by the "unchanging limits" of life and love, the inflexible imperatives of human life. Frank Kermode says: "just as [love] is in its very nature the business of the young, with passions hardly controlled, so it is in its very nature associated with disaster and death". Norman Rabkin says the lovers are doomed by "the self-destructive yearning for annihilation that we recognise as the death-wish".

3. It was just bad luck. Another school of criticism stresses the unfortunate failure of Friar Laurence's message to reach Romeo in Mantua and the calamitous timing of events at the tomb. As L.S. Champion puts it, perhaps "we understand the play better if we think of it as a tragedy of 'bad luck'". To such critics, says Franklin Dickey, the tragedy is flawed because the catastrophe is "embarrassingly fortuitous... the accident of chance to which all human life is subject".

4.   *It was their own fault.* A fourth group argue that we have to blame Romeo and Juliet themselves: they demand too much and defy the rules of society. To these critics the Friar is right: "these violent delights have violent ends". D.A. Stauffer says "the causes of the tragedy lie in the sufferers themselves", whose "dangerous fault... is their extreme rashness".

R.S. White, collecting recent critical approaches to the play, suggests critics fall into one of two camps:

"Throughout the 20th century, criticism of Romeo and Juliet oscillated between [two] poles. At one end lies psychoanalysis, with its belief in the individual psyche, and its assumption that all people are driven from within by universal, primal feelings that seek fulfilment and happiness but are more often than not thwarted, perverted, sublimated into other pursuits, or repressed.

At the other pole lies cultural materialism, which assumes we are driven from without by our circumstances, by chance meetings and random contingencies, by social and cultural attitudes which are unavoidable, by advertising, the sentiments of popular music, family conventions and so on.

At issue are the cherished but contradictory western notions of individualism and of universal human nature. It is significant that defenders of each pole, in their very different ways, deny freedom of choice in our emotional lives. One group asserts that we are compulsively driven and our destinies shaped by largely inherited or manipulated feeling states and expectations, the other that we are at the mercy of the very limited culture of which we have experience."

How does Shakespeare show Juliet's "erotic longing"?

From the moment she commits to her passion, there is a primal demonism in Juliet, reckless, violent, hungry, and strangely carnivalesque. Her big soliloquy in Act Three, Scene Two is the key speech here. when she is patiently awaiting the night to come and her marriage to be consummated. Many readers may have wished that Shakespeare had used some old-fashioned device of soul-struggle, such as the good and bad angel in her ear, causing Juliet to ventriloquise all the things she could never have dreamed of saying. But he doesn't: it is Juliet speaking, very deliberately, and for centuries the fact has caused distress: "the most scandalous obscenity usurps the place of that virgin purity", as A. De Lamartine protested in 1865. De Lamartine's sense of personal affront is understandable, much more so than attempts to pretend that the speech isn't "outrageous" or to euphemise it by patronising appeals to "adolescent energy" or "youthful impatience" (as though to say she doesn't know what she means) or even "ecstasy", with its suggestion of out-of-body experience. And it is surely better that the audience feel the offence than for the offending passages to be cut, as they still often are in productions today.

"We might compare Juliet's words with the mad songs and discourse of Ophelia, with their unwonted bawdy and hints of repressed longings. But Juliet's speech is different – it isn't fractured and nostalgic, but rip-roaringly hungry, racing into commission of the longed-for act. The sexual puns rise thick and fast, as though from suddenly awoken flesh, a flesh that speaks through her, that has taken her tongue hostage. But she intends every word:

> *Spread thy close curtain, love-performing night,*
> *That runaway's eyes may wink, and Romeo*
> *Leap to these arms untalk'd-of and unseen.*
> *Lovers can see to do their amorous rites [3.2]*

This is the consummation of Juliet's identification with the "cheek of night". She calls upon night to cover everything, so that no one will see them have sex. Equally, the "close curtain" she longs to "spread" is her own – her legs and, more to the point, her labia. She is coming into adulthood, piece by piece, looking pitilessly at what she is about to perform, the maidenhood she is set to lose, and saying "come" – she says the word six times, and each time with the full sense of arrival leading to orgasm. (That the one who finally "comes" is the Nurse is a nice piece of bathos.) The fact that she is 13 makes it at once monstrous – in the sense of a strange possession – and awesome – in the sense of precociously sublime, as she is taken over by forces that dwarf her education.

Mercutio has just died, and as I have suggested, much of his demonic energy passes into Juliet. They have always shared astonishing velocity, and this ecstatic speech is Juliet's answer to or echo of Queen Mab, likewise in league with the under-spirits that carry desire beyond all formal or social boundaries and into our very bodies. But then even this explanation seems protective of her willfulness.

For as much as Juliet is taken over by sexual imagination, as much as every image turns into delicious obscenity – as though every last object in the world is suddenly sexualised – we can still hear *her* speaking. Witness the mischievous ironies ("runaways' eyes may wink"), or her subverting and transforming of musty authority:

> *Come civil night*
> *Thou sober-suited Matron all in black,*
> *And learn me how to lose a winning match,*
> *Play'd for a pair of stainless maidenhoods. [3.2]*

She imagines the old tutor as a widow in mourning, the "sober" backdrop to her youthful intoxication. But in Juliet's vision even the old and forgotten are newly enfranchised in sexual delight: "learne me", she says – principally teach me, but also implicitly

learn from me, in that she and her beau will enact a
pattern for the universe:

Give me my Romeo; and when I shall die,
Take him and cut him out in little stars,
And he will make the face of heaven so fine,
That all the world will be in Love with night. [3.2]

This exultant image is at once very simple and
promiscuously suggestive. She is saying give me
him, and produces a scene ecstatically
correspondent to the joy she anticipates, a world
somehow exploding with endlessly reconfigured
Romeos (images like this, and her earlier one of
the lightning, probably suggested the repeated
scenes of fireworks in the night-sky in Baz
Luhrmann's film). It is characteristic that in the
phrase, "when I shall die", the sexual meaning of
"die" is primary rather than dependent: it means
"have sex" (if not necessarily female orgasm). So,
she imagines lying back and seeing the sky aflame
with "little stars", each of them a fraction or glisten
of Romeo. He is at once gone from her, his essence
fissured into de-individuated multiplicity, and still
at her beck and call, still pleasing her as his beauty
hangs above her. Rather than being "shot" into
oblivion, like we might imagine sperm, her lover is
re-composed in the act: "take him and cut him
out". He is at her direction, putty in her hands – or
perhaps like a folded sheet of paper, which the

dexterous girl can transform, with her craft and her scissors, into numerous "little stars".

Juliet is here given one of Shakespeare's great imaginings of sex. We see this in the spaciousness of the image; something deliberate in its making, as she directs it to happen and then watches, half-out of her own body, as it does; the unfolding repetitions, shapes within shapes, that magical sense of a world slowed to one's own pulse and extended beyond normal possibility; the intense wistfulness that wishes the moment longer, somehow knows that it is longer than its "actual" occurrence; an extensive intensity that connects to things and survives in things which the daily world, with its "garish Sun", knows next to nothing about; even, perhaps, a melancholy anticipation that the boy, having brought her to this little death, will leave. All of this works to evoke, I think, the female orgasm (as Romeo is restlessly thinking about getting up...)

As anyone familiar with his sonnets knows, Shakespeare very often identifies erotic longing with deeply destructive instincts. Julie Kristeva suggests that "the shattered, murdered solar metaphor displays Juliet's unconscious desire to break up Romeo's body". Certainly much of the speech, like much of the play, can seem like a testcase proving the coalition of Eros and Thanatos, sex and death. Hugh Grady counters that Juliet's "violence resonates more with the

urgency of desire than with a desire for murder",
seeing in her desire a reflection of "utopian"
possibility that can survive the blank fact of death .
This is certainly part of it. Nonetheless, there are
undeniably demonic and even vampiric shades to
Juliet's sexuality. Her alliance with "loving black-
brow'd night" makes her confederacy with the
dark side pretty clear – a hint made manifest by
Romeo's words over the apparently dead Juliet in
the catacomb:

> *Shall I believe*
> *that unsubstantial Death is amorous,*
> *And that the lean abhorred monster keeps*
> *Thee here in dark to be his paramour? [5.3]*

There is something in Juliet's great soliloquy
which "knows" – as it were before knowing – that
sex involves congress with animalism (the
insistent hawking and hunting images); that it
implies rational as well as physical abandon; that it
is jealous and hungry; that it is sort of stupid, in its
multiple abdications, and yet crafty, in that the eye
is always on the target and obstructions are there
to be avoided; that it turns the normal world into a
facade, one that presents a false face of propriety
and sociality, when in fact the true face is leering,
panting, hot, in anguish; that compulsive punning
may well be the truest mode of speech, as every
object one sees gets turned into a sexual

complement or conspirator; that our day-life, dressed, polite, efficient, at once securely named and essentially anonymous, is a bleached pretence; that it cannot rest, or not for long, in a cosy satisfied hug; that if it is perverse to think of mutilating your lover at the moment of greatest intimacy, it is because sex is constitutionally perverse: for it rehearses all the final things we can never else survive.

Is there a moral in this play?

A young and beautiful couple, wrenched apart by bad luck, would rather die for their love than live apart. The tale is so familiar as almost to neuter criticism. But what are we supposed to think about it? "I think that I speak for more than myself when I assert that the love shared by Romeo and Juliet is as healthy and normative a passion as Western literature affords us", writes Harold Bloom in *Shakespeare: The Invention of the Human* (1998). The French critic Saint-Marc Girardin took a very different view in 1844, arguing that it was peculiarly English to turn *Romeo and Juliet* into such a gloomy tale:

> There is in English literature a very singular taste for death... the young and beautiful Juliet,

before taking the sleeping draught, does not think of Romeo and Romeo alone, who is to come and deliver her from the tomb; her love never enters her thoughts, but she dwells with terror on the funeral vault in which she must be laid, on that abode of death and ghosts; she describes the frenzy which may seize her, and how she may profane the bones of her ancestors... As long as the story of Romeo and Juliet was confined to the circle of Italian literature, those vague and gloomy fancies... were unknown.

As the lovers head toward catastrophe, a powerfully gothic, grotesque, even demonic quality increasingly takes over. In a scene entirely of Shakespeare's invention, he has Paris and Romeo meet at Juliet's tomb. Paris's lament is delicate:

Sweet flower, with flowers thy bridal bed I strew.
O woe, thy canopy is dust and stones
Which with sweet water nightly I will dew... [5.3]

He is careful about the sacred site, careful not to be seen trespassing, careful of invasion, careful too of the place's own youthful vulnerability.

Under yond yew trees lay thee all along,
Holding thy ear close to the hollow ground;
So shall no foot upon the churchyard tread,

Being loose, unfirm, with digging up of graves,
But thou shalt hear it. [5.3]

There is no satire here at all. Shakespeare takes pains to portray a deeply sensitive sensibility. This sacred ground is not, for Paris, guilty of or greedy for the corpses it hides. Instead, the earth itself is invaded, made weaker ("unfirm") by the sorry penetration of the dead. The natural world imagined by Paris, quite unlike Romeo's or Juliet's, is delicate and young, to be aided in its hopes of growth or survival. There is real ecological feeling in his "obsequies", at one with his feeling for the too-soon defeated Juliet.

HOW EXCEPTIONAL ARE THE LOVERS?

Shakespeare gives us a play in which everyone is doomed to irretrievable loss and failure. The examples of the prematurely slain include Mercutio, Tybalt, Paris, Juliet, Romeo, even Lady Montague; Benvolio and the Nurse are likewise abandoned, their carefully etched interests cast aside as useless, irrelevant, or culpable (in the sources the Nurse is banished for hiding the marriage from Juliet's parents; Shakespeare dismisses her, as though of no interest, once she has betrayed Juliet by her casual advocacy of bigamy and led the wailing for the not-dead Juliet). The lovers are partly so moving because, as much as they achieve their truth in

There is the most violent contrast when Romeo enters. He speaks entirely of alienation from both humanity and earth, with eyes only for his deadly target: "Give me that Mattocke, and the wrenching Iron." All the world and everything in it is an obstacle to be overcome; he is like a mandrake come to life, from very bitterness feeding death with more death: "Thou detestable maw, thou womb of death..."

So, what is the moral status of the lovers? Is it even a worthwhile question? The Protestant viewpoint, more or less orthodox in Shakespeare's day, is pretty clear; witness the prefatory "Address to the Reader" in Shakespeare's main source:

opposition to all that surrounds them, they are also the most perfect extension of their world. If they were truly exceptional, they could not be tragic. Consequently, we are rarely on safe ground dismissing one figure or completely trusting another – even Juliet can embarrass her fervent admirers with her erratic conceits, compulsive wordplay, and ghoulish violence. Elsewhere the wisest words can seem strangely unwelcome, at odds with the momentum or emotions of a scene. This often happens with the Friar. We may resent his warnings, or close our ears to them, at the same time as accept their truth or suspect that they will indeed come true. It is too easy – albeit probably irresistible – earnestly to take sides and relish our resentments, to see the lovers as our avatars and everyone else as the preventers and not the prevented. For the play's minor figures too are our proxies. We are all – let us not forget it – the prevented. ◆

And to this ende (good reader) is this tragicall matter written, to describe unto thee a coople of unfortunate lovers, thralling themselves to unhonest desire, neglecting the authorities and advise of parents and frendes, conferring their principall counsels with drunken gossyppes, and superstitious friers (the naturally fitte instruments of unchastitie) attempting all adventures of peryll, for thattaynyng of their wishes lust, using auricular confession (the kay of whoredome, and treason) for furtheraunce of theyr purpose, abusing the honourable name of lawefull marriage, the cloke the shame of stolne contracts, finallye, by all meanes of unhonest lyfe, hasting to most unhappy death. (Arthur Brooke's *The Tragicall Historye of Romeus and Juliet*)

We might think such stuff has nothing to do with any tale ever written for purposes of pleasure; and clearly it is written from a vehement anti-Catholic position – the contempt for friars and condemnation of confession – which Shakespeare is unlikely to have shared. Indeed the tale that Brooke goes on to unfold fails to live up to this trenchant moral intolerance. But let us not forget, either, that the lovers' moments of greatest delight are underpinned by doom. It is as though Shakespeare is constantly whispering in the margins, reminding us not to trust too much, never to forget, to open our eyes, to see that sacrifices are necessary, that the powers they seek to defy – family, society, even night and day and the minute-by-minute clock – will exact their own payback.

Clearly it isn't good enough to gloss the lovers' story simply as one of "prevented love" or "frustrated idealism". Shakespeare adds much to the sources to give the lovers their own space, time, and motion, but also their own ethical world, as though playing by private self-cocooned rules. The effect is not to represent them as "bad" in terms of disobedience or deception; it is not that we are asked to retain allegiance to an order (of behaviour, hierarchy etc.) that the lovers abjure. Rather their commitment to themselves involves the efficient destruction of all other relations – if it doesn't kill them outright, it utterly ends their life with or for Juliet and Romeo. The young couple do this knowingly, with eyes open, yet without a thought for the cost in suffering.

The Danish philosopher Kierkegaard, in his *Fear and Trembling*, says of God's injunction to Abraham to sacrifice his son Isaac, that the "ethical is the temptation". He means by this that the ethical thing to do – *not* to murder his boy, *not* to obey a cruel and arbitrary command – is paradoxically a sin, a worldly "temptation". Abraham does not succumb to this temptation, but not out of meek or fearful obedience. He will kill his son, knowing that his son will return to him. It is absurd, but he acts precisely on the strength of this absurd. The absurd, then, is the "absolute", beyond all ethical negotiation. If he is wrong here, then Abraham is, as Kierkegaard has it, "lost". There is the absolute – or there is nothing. In some ways this is the world of Juliet and Romeo. They violate the ruling ethics of their society; although they have nothing to do with a Christian God, they are each other's deity, each other's absolute. But unlike the biblical tale, it is a godless, deathly, tragic absolute. Juliet "dies" to Romeo, but she only returns alive to his death; he dies for her, and can only return to her through the desperate conjoining of her "phallic" suicide.

There is no doubt at all that sympathies lie squarely with the lovers. Even Brooke, in Shakespeare's source, cannot stay true to the moral condemnation which his prologue prepares us to expect. But sympathy and morality can be at odds; intimacy with a character does not necessarily mean approval. And so might it be the case that we are on the lovers' side even as we know, at some level, that they are foolish or wrong or destructive?

Consider poor Lady Montague. She only gets a couple of lines, trying to stop the fight, worrying about her sad son, and then she is absent until in the final scene we hear she has dropped dead from grief. Surely she did not deserve this; surely her son was a grotesque egoist who should have thought more about his mother!

Then again, do we care, really? Any more than

we care about boring Benvolio, who disappears, hardly noticed? I doubt it. We might say here that the play inculcates, or embodies, a terrible self-centredness, in which the presumed "grace" of the lovers allows and forgives anything. What if everyone acted as this pair does? There would be chaos; civilisation could not continue.

But of course such statements are ridiculous and irrelevant. The point of the lovers' rebellion is that almost no one *does* act like this, although almost everyone may have wanted to. The rebellion loses meaning if there are no walls to climb. And the play everywhere knows that life goes on. We survive with barely a thought to the disappearance of Benvolio and the dropping dead of old Lady Montague. We might resent the survival of Lords Capulet and Montague beyond their children, and think their promise of a "statue in pure Gold" a presumptuous irrelevance. But can we really resent the relative indifference of Peter and the three musicians, who enter after the scene of lamentation over Juliet's corpse, play "Heart's ease", exchange a few jokes, and clearly feel more concerned by what they can get away with than any real grief for the dead daughter of the house? Or even the self-protectiveness of the Friar, who covers his ears and runs from the scene, facilitating the suicide of Juliet? We are all at the centre of our own lives. This, as much as anything, is the moral of Romeo and Juliet's passion as well. Who is anyone to exile us from our centres? My love is not his love, her love is not yours. It is right that we should cherish our own, and be permitted in the instinct.

Finally, however, it is clear that social moralism is not the play's endpoint – not even the lesson learnt by the parents about their destructive enmity. More to the point is the sheer imperative that we experience life in the stony face of death. This, I take it, is the meaning of the fathers' shamefaced attempts at reparation; they take their punishment, and we can see in these closing movements: the glazed, shocked attempts of parents trying simply to move in the wake of devastated guilt and grief. For death is the bass-chord and boundary of this play – love is impossible without it, just as a life is. Contrary to popular reputation, *Romeo and Juliet* is not ultimately about believing in love, or wanting to love or to be loved, or identifying one's true love and going for it whatever the cost. If it were, then Shakespeare's initial characterisation of Romeo, in love with Rosaline, spouting lovelorn clichés, would be less satiric, less premature and frankly disappointing than it is.

The point about this first love is precisely that it is too chosen, too much an effect – or affectation – of will. The real thing hits as though by "lightning". It is accidental, in the sense of unplanned and unpredicted. But precisely because it is not willed or even chosen, it becomes as though predestined – as though accidents themselves are providential. It comes from elsewhere; it takes and possesses: the individual is at once helpless and emboldened, raised to their greatest, most purposive height by the recognition of powerlessness in the face of such a force. This is why their love is always couched in metaphors of sun, moon, night and so on. To the extent that Juliet and Romeo are free subjects, they are tiny. Thought is never free in Verona. Juliet and Romeo reject one mode of determinism for another. This is why the work is so large and mythic. The lovers are taken, possessed: they embody the black cosmic comedy of our unfreedom.

A SHORT CHRONOLOGY

1562 Arthur Brooke's 3,000 line poem, *The Tragicall Historye of Romeus and Juliet* (1562), also a source for *The Two Gentlemen of Verona*. There are twelve allusions to Romeo by English writers between 1562 and 1583.

1564 Shakespeare born in Stratford-on-Avon.

1590-92 *Henry VI parts I, II* and *III*.

1593 English translations of two poems by Du Bartas published in John Eliot's *Ortho-Epia Gallica*.

1594 *Love's Labour's Lost*.

1595-6 conventional date of *Richard II* and *A Midsummer Night's Dream*. *Romeo and Juliet*, dated by stylistic resemblance to *Richard II* and *A Midsummer Night's Dream*, is generally thought to have been composed between 1591 (11 years after the Dover Straits earthquake) and 1595. 1596 is the latest possible date, since by March 1597 the play had been performed and sold to a printer. Richard Burbage was probably the first Romeo, and Master Richard Goffe Juliet. The play was immediately successful – on the title page of the first published text it is referred to as one "that hath been often (with great applause) plaid publiquely".

Opposite: Rudolf Nureyev and Margot Fonteyn as Romeo and Juliet in Paul Czinner's 1966 film

1597 *Romeo and Juliet* first appears in print, in an unlicensed quarto edition, possibly assembled by the actors playing Romeo and Paris. A second quarto, "newly corrected, augmented and amended", was published in 1599, probably produced from Shakespeare's rough draft of the play.

1599-1602 *Hamlet, Twelfth Night, Troilus and Cressida*

1603 Elizabeth I dies. accession of James I

1603-1606 *Othello, King Lear, Macbeth, Measure for Measure, Antony and Cleopatra*

1616 23 April Shakespeare dies

1623 publication of a collected edition of Shakespeare's works, including *Romeo and Juliet*; this becomes known as the First Folio.

1662 the great diarist Pepys called it "the play of itself the worst that ever I heard in my life."

1679 Thomas Otway adapted it to a Roman setting – Caius Marius - and had Juliet wake before Romeo dies. This was very successful, and played for over 60 years.

1748 David Garrick's revival, which held the stage for 97 years.

1800s having fallen into disfavour, with Romeo thought too womanish Charlotte Cushman, the great actress, revived it, playing Romeo herself, recovering Shakespeare's plot whilst still leaving out bawdy and lots of small scenes. It became all about her Romeo.

1935 John Gielgud's production, which returned fully to Shakespeare's text. He wanted it to be operatic, so that the lovers "shall sing those marvellous duets while the other characters speak their lines."

1947 Peter Brook's version concentrated on the lovers, "two children caught in the maelstrom around them". Brook's key term was this: "For now, these hot days, is the mad blood stirring..." Brook cut widely, his accent on speed.

BIBLIOGRAPHY

Bloom, H, *Shakespeare: The Invention of the Human*, Fourth Estate, 1998

Giraud, R, "The Passionate Oxymoron in Romeo and Juliet", in his *Mimesis and Theory: Essays on Literature and Criticism*, 1953-2005, Stanford University Press, 2008; A *Theatre of Envy: William Shakespeare*, OUP, 1991

Goldberg, J, *Shakespeare's Hand*, University of Minnesota Press, 2003

Grady, H, *Shakespeare and Impure Ethics*, Cambridge University Press, 2009

Everett, B, "Romeo and Juliet: The Nurse's Story", in *Young Hamlet*, OUP, 1989; sees the nurse not as a prattler, but a central character.

Hegel, G, *Hegel's Aesthetic: Lectures on Fine Art*, vol 1, trans T.M. Knox, OUP 1975

Kahn, C, *Man's Estate: Masculine Identity in Shakespeare*, University of California Press, 1981

Kristeva, J, "Love-Hatred in the Couple" in White, R, *Romeo and Juliet*, Palgrave Macmillian, 2001

Palfrey, S, *Doing Shakespeare* (revised edition), Arden, 2011; especially on the meaning of Mercutio's puns

Palfrey, S and Stern, T, *Shakespeare in Parts*, Oxford, 2007; especially on shared and unshared cues

Porter, J, S*hakespeare's Mercutio: His History and Drama,* Chapel Hill, 1988; extract in White, R, *Romeo and Juliet*, 2001

Ryan, K, *Shakespeare*, Palgrave Macmillan (3rd edn), 2002

Snyder, S, *The Comic Matrix of Shakespeare's Tragedies,* Princeton University Press, 1979

INDEX